THE DYSFUNCTIONAL GOURMET

Recipes For People Just Crazy About Food

by
Bob Fugate

Published by Bob Fugate Creative Marketing, Inc.
© Copyright 2005 by Robert Fugate Jr.

ISBN 0-9771628-0-X

1st Printing September 2005
Printed in the United States of America by:

G&R Publishing Company
507 Industrial Street
Waverly, Iowa 50677
800-383-1679
gandr@gandrpublishing.com
www.gandrpublishing.com

The Dysfunctional Gourmet

Recipes for People Just Crazy About Food

Acknowledgement & Expression of Appreciation

We could not have put this book together without the kind help of all the guards who did everything from smuggling in paper and pencils to testing our recipes.

We'd especially like to thank the bulimics on Ward Seven who devoted so much of their time taste-testing our creations. We smile when we think of how you could sample 75 or 80 creations a day and never seem to get full!

We also owe a special note of thanks to our favorite paranoid schizophrenic, Eddy, who tirelessly proofed this document for errors under the mistaken belief that he would be turned over to a South American torture squad if we found even one little typo. Hey, Eddy! We found a misspelled word on page 87. Pack your sunscreen. (Just kidding!)

And finally, I would like to thank my parents who would have loved to see their son's work in print and the guys of Engine Company 45. Again, I apologize for that sad day last March. I really didn't think such a small kitchen fire would get out of hand so fast. But hey, for once the roast was really done!

Please use these recipes only as directed. Marty, our attorney, asked us to include the following notification to cover our buns. so to speak:

WARNING

These recipes are definitely not for everyone. Don't drink alcohol to a level of intoxication with these recipes. The combination may increase your chances of getting dizzy, married, and/or divorced or may raise your blood pressure. These recipes do not protect a woman or her partner from sexually transmitted diseases, picking out bad wallpaper, nor do they remove your bipolar tendencies.

The most common side effects of these recipes were double vision, single vision, triple vision, headaches, bloating, vomiting, more bloating, diarrhea, gas, foaming at the mouth and upset stomachs. Backache, headache, side ache, heartache and muscle ache were also reported, sometimes with a delayed onset of six to eight years. Most people weren't bothered by the side effects enough to stop eating food. Bon Appetit!

Marty

Read What Others Are Saying About

The Dysfunctional Gourmet
Recipes For People Just Crazy About Food

"I ate everything in the book. I did. No, I really did. I ate it all."
    Monica
    Eating Disorders Unit
    Name of Mental Health Facility Withheld by Request

"Someone put something in my food."
    Eddie
    Last Name Withheld by Request
    Name of Mental Health Facility Withheld by Request

"Please help me get out of here. Great soups."
    John
    Last Name Withheld by Request
    Name of Mental Health Facility Withheld by Request

"I like all of the recipes. But not in one day."
    Amber
    Last Name Withheld by Request
    Name of Mental Health Facility Withheld by Request

"I like food. But I wouldn't hurt it. I mean I wouldn't kill anything, even food."
    Jerry
    Violent Offenders Wing
    Cell 495, Building Three
    Name of Mental Health Facility Withheld by Request

Table of Contents

To make it easier for you, we've grouped our treasure-trove of culinary delights according to clinical diagnosis.

Obsessive Compulsive Kickoffs - Appetizers 1

The Lighter Side of Depression - Soups & Salads 9

Anorexic Tidbits - Vegetables & Side Dishes 25

The Bulimic Buffet - Main Dishes 33

Rising Addictions - Breads & Rolls..45

Schizophrenic Fare - Cakes, Cookies & Just Desserts............................51

Cooking & Nutritional Information

Household Hints

Obsessive Compulsive Kickoffs

Appetizers

CHUCK'S FAVORITE VEGETABLE PIZZA

1 tube crescent roll dough
8 oz. cream cheese, softened
1/2 c. mayonnaise
1 tsp. dill weed
1 T. minced onion

Toppings: (use any) shredded cheese, zucchini, mushrooms, sprouts, broccoli, ham, sunflower seeds, red or green pepper

Wash hands. Spread dough flat on pizza pan. Wash hands. Pinch seams. Wash hands. Bake at 375 for 11 to 13 minutes. Wash hands. Cool. Wash hands. Mix next 4 ingredients and spread over dough. Wash hands. Add chopped and shredded vegetables. Wash hands.

Note: Chuck is both a vegetable and a vegetable lover. This is his favorite!

PERFECTLY ROUND PARTY CHEESE BALLS

1/2 c. butter, softened
2 - 8 oz. cream cheese, softened
4 oz. bleu cheese
1 to 2 T. finely chopped onion
1/2 c. chopped ripe olives
1/2 c. chopped walnuts

Blend first three ingredients. Add remaining ingredients and mix. Chill overnight. Shape into 2 balls. No, round balls! I mean perfectly round balls. Roll in chopped nuts or parsley. Those aren't perfectly round. If they aren't perfectly round something bad will happen. Round! If they aren't perfectly round something bad will happen. I warned you.

CORN & BLACK BEAN SALSA

10 oz. package frozen corn, thawed, drained well
1 red or green pepper, diced (or combination)
1 small red onion, diced (or green onions)
1/4 c. minced fresh cilantro (or 1 T. dried)
3 T. olive oil
Grated zest and juice of one lime
2 T. cider vinegar
1 tsp. salt
1/4 tsp. cayenne pepper
1/2 of 15 oz. can black beans, rinsed and drained

Combine all. Refrigerate to blend flavors. But what shelf should you put them on? The top shelf. But wait. That might not be lucky. Better put them on the bottom shelf. Wait. That dish isn't lined up with the milk carton. Better put them on the middle shelf and make sure that all of the labels in your refrigerator are facing to the front. Exactly to the front. I don't want you leaving the house until they all are perfect. Serve with tortilla chips.

ODD-EVEN CORN RELISH

16 oz. frozen corn, defrosted in microwave
1/4 c. red and green pepper, chopped
1/4 c. green onion, sliced
3 T. cider vinegar
1 T. olive oil
1/4 tsp. sugar
1/4 to 1/2 tsp. salt
Several dashes of red pepper sauce

Count the corn kernels in the bag of frozen corn. If it is an odd number proceed. If it is an even number recount the kernels in the bag of frozen corn. If it is still an odd number proceed. If it is an even number recount the kernels in the bag of frozen corn. Now eat one and count the corn kernels in the bag of frozen corn. Then chop the red and green peppers so that they are exactly the same size as the green onions you chop. Combine all and chill to blend flavors.

ON AND OFF CRANBERRY SALSA

1 1/2 c. fresh or frozen cranberries
1/3 c. sugar
2 green onions, chopped
1/4 c. chopped fresh cilantro
Juice and zest of 1 lime
1 jalapeno, seeded and minced
2 tsp. chopped fresh ginger
1/8 tsp. salt

In food processor, add all. Pulse on and off until uniformly chopped but still textured. Pulse on and off. Spoon it into serving bowl. Cover and chill 2 to 8 hours to let flavors blend. Serve with cheese and crackers.

If you see someone without a smile –
Give him one of yours.

EASY PATE'

8 oz. braunschweiger
8 oz. cream cheese, softened
4 T. onion, finely chopped
1 tsp. lemon juice
1 tsp. Worcestershire
Dash of salt and pepper

Mix all thoroughly. Spoon into a small bowl and chill. While chilling, line up your cookbooks alphabetically according to size. Now alphabetize by author. Next, rearrange your soup cans according to food group. Now check the expiration dates on everything in your refrigerator and then rearrange so that oldest items are on the top shelf, arranged front to back, and the newest items are on the bottom shelf, also arrange front to back. When ready to serve, count out an even number of crackers and arrange on plate, making sure your Easy Pate' is centered exactly in the middle.

THE LOCKED WARD'S FAVORITE PARTY MIX

4 c. each: dry roast peanuts; short pretzels; garlic bread sticks, broken; small round pretzels, oyster crackers
2 c. each: rice chex, corn chex, and wheat chex
2 c. oil
2 packages ranch dressing mix
1 tsp. dill weed
1 tsp. dill seed
1 T. garlic salt

Mix oil and seasonings. Pour over remaining ingredients. Cover and let sit overnight, stirring occasionally.

Note: This is a big favorite on the locked ward. It not only tastes great but the little chex pieces can be counted again and again or traded for cigarettes.

A recipe that is as old as time itself,
Yet always delightful,
They call it simply friendship;
Beloved, tried and true.

LAYERED CAVIAR DIP

5 hard-cooked eggs, finely chopped, finely chopped, finely chopped, finely chopped, finely chopped, finely chopped, finely chopped, finely chopped, finely chopped, finely chopped, finely chopped, finely chopped, finely chopped, finely chopped, finely chopped, finely chopped, finely chopped

2 green onions, finely chopped, finely chopped, finely chopped, finely chopped, finely chopped, finely chopped, finely chopped, finely chopped, finely chopped, finely chopped, finely chopped, finely chopped

1 1/2 c. sour cream
2 jars (4oz.) black caviar (drained)
Juice of 1 lemon

In 8-inch shallow glass dish, layer eggs and green onion, then spread on sour cream to cover. Carefully spoon on the caviar. Squeeze lemon juice over all. Serve chilled or at room temperature with small toasts.

SPOTLESS CHICKEN LIVER PATE

1 onion, chopped
1 lb chicken livers, cleaned, trimmed
1/2 lb butter, softened
1 tsp. cognac
1 tsp. 5 spice powder

1/2 tsp. salt
1/8 tsp. pepper
1/2 c. whipping cream, whipped
1/4 tsp. ground cloves

Wash hands for 6.5 minutes. Sauté onion and livers in 2 T. butter 4 to 5 minutes until livers are firm and pink in center. Wash hands for 13 minutes. Cool. Wash hands for 2.8 minutes. Food process liver, butter and seasonings. Wash hands for 45 seconds. Chill 15 minutes. Stir and chill 15 more minutes. Wash hands for 12 minutes. Whip cream and fold in. Wash hands for 4.5 minutes. Chill.

If you wait for perfect conditions,
You will never get anything done.

TIMELESS PEACH SALSA

2 c. diced peaches
1/2 c. red onion, diced
1/2 c. red bell pepper, diced
1/2 tsp. jalapeno, minced
2 tsp. olive oil

2 T. limejuice
3 T. minced cilantro
1 tsp. salt
3 T. balsamic vinegar (optional)

Combine all ingredients. Refrigerate 1 hour or let stand 30 minutes at room temperature. 30 minutes is the same as 1800 seconds. How many times can you blink in 1800 seconds? Count them while you are waiting. Makes 3 cups

OVERNIGHT VEGETABLE DIP

8 oz. sour cream
1/3 c. mayonnaise

1 package Italian dressing mix

Blend, lock doors, chill overnight. Good night. Did you lock the doors? Okay, good night. Did you lock all of them? Okay, good night. Are you sure? Okay, good night. Did you lock the doors? Okay, good night. Did you lock all of them? Okay, good night. Are you sure? Okay, good night. What was that? Good night. Did you lock the doors? Okay, good night. Did you lock all of them? Okay, good night. Are you sure? Okay, good night. What was that? Good night. Did you lock the doors? Okay, good night. Did you lock all of them? Okay, good night. Are you sure? Okay, good night. What was that?

APPETIZER QUICHE

1 box refrigerated piecrusts or dough
   for two-crust pie
4 eggs
2 c. half & half
1 1/2 c. shredded cheese

1/2 lb bacon, cooked & crumbled
1/4 c. chopped onion, sautéed
Salt and pepper to taste
Dash nutmeg

Fit crusts into a 10 by 15 inch jelly roll pan and pinch seams firmly. Count all of the pans in your kitchen. Bake at 425 degrees for 12 to 15 minutes until lightly browned. Count all of your forks. Cool. Lower oven temp to 325. Sprinkle cheese, bacon and onion over crusts. Whisk remaining ingredients together and pour in baked crust. Count all of your spoons. Bake 20 to 25 minutes until filling appears set when gently shaken. If it puffs, poke with fork to allow air to escape. Count all of your knives. Serve warm or at room temperature. Serves 12+ if you are into counting things.

STEVE'S ARTICHOKE DIP

10 oz. can artichoke hearts, drained and chopped
1/2 c. green onions, chopped
1 c. grated cheddar cheese
1 c. grated Swiss cheese
3/4 c. mayonnaise
1/2 tsp. pepper

Wash the windows again. Preheat oven to 400 degrees. Wash hands. In large bowl, chop artichoke hearts. Re-arrange your sock drawer. Stir in remaining ingredients. Count linoleum squares on kitchen floor. Spread into 8x8" dish or pie plate. Alphabetize CDs. Bake 10-20 minutes, until bubbling. Line up fringe on all of the rugs in your house. Serve with bagel chips or crackers. Scrape paint dots off all of your floor moldings.

Note: My friend Steve has a head that is shaped just like an artichoke. We named this dish after him.

CRACKLESS BUFFALO CHICKEN WINGS

2 1/2 lbs chicken wings (about 12 to 15)
Sauce
1/4 c. red-hot sauce
1/2 c. melted butter
A splash of vinegar

Go to the store and buy chicken wings. Park so that your car is not touching any lines. Do not step on cracks in the pavement while walking into and out of the store. Take the wings home. Do not park your car on any cracks. Bring wings into kitchen without stepping anywhere except in the exact center of your floor tiles Deep-fry wings at 400 degrees for about 12 minutes or until crispy. Dip wings in sauce and serve. Or bake wings on rack in pan at 425 degrees for around 1 hour, turning halfway through cooking time.

If you tell the truth, you never
Have to remember what you said.

VERY COMPLICATED CHEESE & SPINACH PUFFS

10 oz. frozen chopped spinach
1/2 c. chopped onion
2 eggs
1/2 c. shredded cheddar
1/3 c. bleu cheese salad dressing
2 T. melted butter
1/4 tsp. garlic powder
8 1/2 oz. package corn muffin mix
Dijon mustard for serving

Cook spinach with onion as directed on package. Better read those directions again. Drain and squeeze dry. Better read those directions again. In medium bowl, beat eggs. Better read those directions again. Add remaining ingredients and mix well. Better read those directions again. Chill for 1 hour or until easy to handle. Better read those directions again. Better yet, call toll-free hotline number on bag for more directions. Shape 1-inch balls and arrange on greased cookie sheets. Better read those directions again. Bake at 350 for 10 to 15 minutes or until lightly browned. (Frozen puffs 18 to 20 minutes.) Better read those directions again. Better yet, call toll-free hotline number on bag again for even more detailed directions. Serve warm with mustard. Don't screw this up!

OUR FAVORITE DAY ROOM CHILI DIP

6 to 8 oz. cream cheese, softened
15 oz. can chili, no beans
2 c. shredded cheese
Chopped black olives
Chives for garnish

Spread cream cheese in glass pie plate. Spoon chili over and sprinkle with cheese. Microwave 8 to 10 minutes. Garnish with olives and chives. Serve with taco chips.

Note: We have this dip in our day room all of the time. Even the catatonic patients perk up when this one comes in on the med cart.

ROAST BEEF & HORSERADISH SPIRALS

8 oz. cream cheese, softened
2 scallions, chopped, about 1/2 cup
1/4 c. fresh parsley, chopped
1 T. horseradish, drained
1/4 tsp. garlic powder
1/4 tsp. salt
2 - 10 inch flour tortillas
8 oz. deli sliced roast beef

Combine first 6 ingredients. Spread cheese mixture on both tortillas. Top with beef, leaving a 1/2-inch border around edges. Roll up tightly, wrap in plastic wrap. Chill until firm. Slice diagonally into ½ inch slices. Make sure the slices are ALL exactly ½ inch. Do not eat any that are 7/16 or less. Also do not eat any that are 9/16 or greater. Remember: do not eat any that are 7/16 or less. Also do not eat any that are 9/16 or greater. If you do, well, it's on you, buddy.

BETTY'S EXTRA SPARKLY SPINACH DIP

1 c. mayonnaise
1 c. sour cream
1 package spinach, thawed and drained
1 T. parmesan cheese
1 package vegetable soup mix
Hawaiian bread

Clean the kitchen floor. Mix dip ingredients. Clean the kitchen floor again. Chill to blend flavors. Missed a spot. Clean the kitchen floor again. Hollow out the Hawaiian bread and fill with dip. Clean the kitchen floor again. Why is it that your friend Donna has twice as many kids and yet her floors are just so much cleaner? Sad.

LUCKY POT STICKERS

1 c. minced or ground pork
1 minced green onion
2 T. soy sauce
1/2 tsp. sugar
1/2 tsp. sherry
1 T. cornstarch
1/2 tsp. dark sesame oil
Won ton wrappers

Tap your forehead seven times for luck. Combine filling ingredients. Dot won ton wrapper with 2 tsp. filling. Tap your forehead seven more times. Wet edges and pinch close, or use a won ton press. Tap your forehead seven times seven minus four. Heat 1 T. oil in large frying pan. Brown pot stickers in one layer over medium heat until bottoms are golden, 8 to 10 minutes. Reduce heat to low, pour 1/3 c. chicken broth in pan. Tap your forehead seven times only this time use the correct fingers. Cover and steam 10 minutes. Uncover and cook until all liquid is absorbed. Check windows for signs of forced entry.

PERFECT REUBEN DIP

6 oz. corned beef, diced
1 c. sauerkraut, rinsed and drained
8 oz. cream cheese, softened
6 oz. shredded Swiss cheese
2 T. Thousand Island Dressing

Line up all of your forks on the kitchen table. Make sure they point true North. Use a compass. Mix sauerkraut, cream cheese and Swiss cheese. Add corned beef and dressing. Microwave, or put in Crockpot and heat on low until cheeses are melted, stirring occasionally. Serve warm with rye cocktail bread or rye crackers. Put all of the forks away except one. Carry this one with you for luck.

The Lighter Side of Depression

Soups & Salads

WHITE BEAN SAD SOUP

1 large onion, chopped
3 cloves garlic, minced
2 carrots, chopped
14 oz. can chicken broth
3/4 tsp. dried sage
1/2 tsp. dried marjoram
1 can canillini beans, drained
10 oz. package frozen chopped kale or spinach
1/4 tsp. salt
1/2 tsp. pepper
Parmesan cheese

Sauté onion, carrots and garlic in 1 T. olive oil until almost tender. Burst into tears. Add 1/2 c. broth and seasonings, cover and simmer 5 or 10 minutes until carrots are tender. Burst into tears some more. Add remaining ingredients and simmer 10 more minutes. Cry uncontrollably. Sprinkle bowls with parmesan if desire. Serves 4

Note: I call this my Sad Soup because we were eating it the night our dog was run over by a street sweeper.

HAPPY FAMILY THREE-BEAN SOUP

1 lb bulk sausage
1 lg onion, chopped
4 cloves garlic, minced
19 oz. can white kidney beans
15 oz. can black beans, drained
14 oz. can (or less) chicken broth
1 package (9 oz.) frozen green beans
1/2 tsp. thyme
1/4 tsp. ground red pepper

Brown sausage. In 2 T. fat, sauté onion and garlic until soft. Feel hopeless. Puree white beans, undrained. Feel hopeless some more. Add to pan with remaining ingredients. Resign yourself to a life of loneliness. Simmer 5 minutes. Serves 6

Note: Most happy families have three people in them and that is why we have named this Happy Three Bean soup. Of course, you can eat it alone. It will be sad, but you can do it.

LOST LOVE BEAN SOUP

6 oz. sausage, sliced thin
3 c. cabbage, chopped
11 oz. can bean with bacon soup
11 oz. can tomato soup
1 T. dried onion flakes
1 c. water

Combine all ingredients in a medium saucepan and think about all of the places you've never been to. Simmer 15 minutes. Do you think you'd be traveling more if you hadn't blown your marriage to that wonderful guy? Sure you would. Serves 6 normal, happy people or one depressive individual who will never have a normal life. Mother was right, you were wrong, get over it.

TEARS IN MY TACO SOUP

2 lbs hamburger
1 onion, chopped
15 oz. can pinto beans, undrained
15 oz. can kidney beans, undrained
16 oz. can corn, undrained
28 oz. can diced tomatoes w/green chilies

1 package taco seasoning mix
1 package dry ranch dressing mix
1 c. beef stock
8 oz. cream cheese

Brown hamburger and onions. Add all but the cream cheese and simmer, uncovered, one hour. While simmering, think about the poor migrant workers who are being exploited. Add cream cheese and heat through. Enjoy it you big pig.

CHUNKY BEAN AND VEGETABLE SOUP

2 T. olive oil
2 celery stalks, chopped
2 leeks, sliced
3 carrots, sliced
2 garlic cloves, crushed
14 oz. can crushed tomatoes with basil

1 quart vegetable or chicken stock
14 oz. can cannelloni beans, drained
1 T. pesto sauce
Salt, pepper to taste
Parmesan cheese for garnish

Feeling empty? Heat olive oil in large saucepan. Add celery, leeks, carrots and garlic and cook slowly for about 5 minutes until they are soft. Still feel empty? Stir in tomatoes and stock and bring to a boil. Lower heat, cover and simmer for 15 minutes. Got a lump in your throat? Stir in the beans and pesto, season. Heat through 5 minutes longer. Still feel empty? Serves 4 people or one big loser who feels empty.

Looking on the bright side of life
Never causes eye strain.

CREAMED CABBAGE SOUP

2 c. shredded cabbage
1 medium onion, diced
3/4 stick butter
1/2 tsp. salt
1/2 tsp. pepper

1/2 tsp. caraway seeds
2 T. flour
3 c. milk
1/4 c. parmesan cheese
1/2 lb smoked sausage, sliced

Sauté onions and cabbage in butter until cabbage wilts. Are you a burden to others? Add seasoning, cover and simmer 15 to 20 minutes until cabbage is tender. Add flour, stir well and cook 2 to 3 minutes on low. Add milk, bring to boiling and stir one minute. Add sausage and warm through. Are you sure you're not a burden to others? They probably won't come right out and tell you. Sprinkle with cheese and weep. Serves 6 They never come right out and tell you. They just call less often and then simply disappear.

ALL GONE CURRIED BUTTERNUT SQUASH SOUP

3 lb butternut squash, peeled, cut in chunks
1 med. onion, chopped
1/4 tsp. cayenne pepper

1 1/2 tsp. curry powder
3 1/2 c. chicken stock
1/4 c. yogurt or heavy cream to finish

Sauté onion in 1 T. olive oil until soft. Stir in cayenne and curry. Add squash and broth. Bring to boil, cover and reduce heat to medium low. Simmer 20-30 minutes until squash is tender. Puree. Season with salt if needed. Add about 1/4 c. cream before serving. Or add a swirl to each bowl. Gosh that swirl looks so sad. And soon it will be all gone. Life is that way. Soon it will be all gone and no one will remember you. Serves 6.

LIMA BEAN AND BACON SOUP WITH A FROWN

2 slices lean bacon
1 small onion, chopped
2 c. beef broth

10 oz. package frozen lima beans
1/2 c. heavy cream

Cook bacon until crisp. Drain and crumble. Sauté onion in remaining fat. Add broth, beans and half the bacon and simmer, covered, for 15 to 20 minutes or until beans are tender. Puree mixture with the cream. Garnish with remaining bacon. Remember how much you used to enjoy this soup? And now, well, it just seems so sad. Come to think of it, everything seems sad. Serves 2 if you can dig up a friend.

WE HEARD THIS IS THE POPE'S FAVORITE SOUP

1 pound bulk Italian sausage, browned, drained
3 large russet potatoes, diced
1 large onion, chopped
1/2 can bacon bits
2 cloves garlic, minced
2 c. kale, Swiss chard, or chopped spinach
6 c. chicken stock
1 c. heavy cream
1/2 tsp. salt
Pepper and cayenne pepper to taste

Place onions, potatoes, chicken stock and garlic in pot. Cook on medium heat until potatoes are tender. Add sausage, bacon and seasonings. Simmer 10 minutes. Add kale and cream and heat through. Serves one Pope or 6 sinners. Have you sinned? Maybe that is why you feel so sad. Maybe you are being paid back for all of those rotten things you did as a teenager.

CRYING IN MY BEER CHEESE SOUP

4 c. milk
1 1/2 tsp. salt
1/4 tsp. garlic salt
1/8 tsp. white pepper
1/2 c. butter
3/4 c. flour
8 oz. cheese whiz
4 oz. beer (or more to thin)
Popped corn for garnish

If drinking doesn't help, maybe this will. Warm cheese whiz. Make roux with butter and flour. Warm milk to simmer and add seasonings. Whisk in enough roux to thicken. Add cheese whiz and whisk thoroughly. Stir in beer. Now have a good cry in your beer cheese soup. Serves 4

Yesterday is history,
Tomorrow is a mystery,
Today is a gift.
That's why we call it the Present.

SUNNY CARIBBEAN VEGETABLE SOUP

2 T. butter
1 onion, chopped
1 garlic clove, minced
2 carrots, sliced
2 medium potatoes, diced
1 cup leftover pork roast

1 1/2 quarts vegetable or chicken stock
2 bay leaves
1/2 tsp. dried thyme leaves
1/2 tsp. Caribbean jerk seasoning
Salt & red pepper, to taste

Melt butter. Don't you wish the sun would come out today? Add onion, garlic, carrots and potatoes and sauté for a few minutes until they begin to soften. It's okay to cry while you add the stock, bay leaves, thyme and pork and bring to a boil. Life is so sad. Season and simmer for 25 minutes or until vegetables are tender. Serve with chopped green onion as garnish. Serves 6

Note: Sad people rarely live as long as happy people—even when they eat well. Don't buy any green bananas.

ALONE AGAIN WITH MY MULLIGATAWNY SOUP

1/2 c. each: onion and celery, carrot, diced
1/4 c. butter or olive oil
1 1/2 T. flour
2 tsp. curry powder
4 c. chicken broth
1/4 c. diced tart apple

1/2 c. cooked rice
1/2 c. diced cooked chicken
1 tsp. salt
1/4 tsp. pepper
1/8 tsp. thyme
1/2 c. cream

Sauté vegetables in butter. Stir in flour and curry powder. Cook about 3 minutes and add broth. Simmer 30 minutes. Add rice, chicken, apples and seasonings and simmer 15 more minutes. Stir in cream before serving. Serves 4. Do you have that many friends? No, I mean real friends? Many times the people that you think are your friends—really aren't your friends at all. They are just using you. Are they worth sharing this soup with? Probably not. Take the phone off the hook.

CHICKEN NOT SO WILD RICE SOUP

1 chicken breast, cooked and diced
1/2 c. each: onion, celery, carrots and mushrooms
3 T. butter
1/2 c. flour

3 c. chicken broth
2 c. cooked wild rice
1/2 tsp. salt
1 c. half & half
2 T. dry sherry

Sauté vegetables in butter. Turn the phone ringer off. Pour yourself a stiff drink. Stir in flour, add broth and bring to boil. Shut the drapes. Stir in rice and chicken and simmer 5 minutes. Turn off the lights and don't answer the door. Stir in cream and sherry and season. Cry. Heat through. Drink. Go to back to bed for the rest of the day. Serves 6

CRAWL SPACE CHEESE TORTELLINI PASTA SALAD

1 lg (5 servings) and 1 small fresh cheese tortellini
1/3 bottle zesty Italian dressing
1/3 small bottle Balsamic dressing
Salt and pepper to taste
8 oz. pitted Kalamata olives (or ripe olives)

3/4 package baby spinach leaves
Small jar roasted red pepper, drained and chopped
1/2 small red onion, thinly sliced
4 oz. crumbled tomato-basil feta cheese

If you can drag yourself out of bed, cook cheese tortellini according to package directions, drain and cool. Combine all ingredients. Season to taste. Refrigerate a few hours before serving. Doesn't the time drag? Did you ever notice how a few hours seem like an eternity? Especially when absolutely no one cares about you. No one. Count the number of other people who are as lonely as you are today. Now go hide in the crawl space with a nice plate of pasta.

The love in your heart wasn't put there to stay;
Love isn't love until you give it away.

ALMOST AS GOOD AS YOUR SISTER'S GERMAN POTATO SALAD

6 medium potatoes
6 slices bacon
3/4 c. chopped onion
2 T. flour
1/4 c. sugar
1 tsp. salt
1/2 tsp. celery seed
1/2 tsp. pepper
3/4 c. water
1/3 c. vinegar
2 T. snipped parsley

Peel and cut potatoes into bite-sized pieces and boil until tender. Drain. In a large skillet, fry bacon, remove, drain and crumble. Sauté onions in bacon drippings until golden. Are you tired? Blend in flour, sugar, salt, pepper and celery seed until smooth and bubbly. Too bad life isn't smooth for you. Your sister sure is doing well. Add water and vinegar and cook; boil one minute. Combine all. Remember that song about the man who left his wife? Try and remember the lyrics while you bake this in a 2 qt. casserole at 325 degrees until heated through, about 35-40 minutes. Serve 6

SEMI-VIOLENT HOLIDAY CRANBERRY SALAD

3 oz. cream cheese
1 16 oz. can whole cranberry sauce
1 to 2 c. whipped topping
2 c. mini marshmallows
Chopped walnuts, optional

Beat cream cheese until softened, really beat it! Then beat in the cranberries. Fold in the whipped topping, mini marshmallows and walnuts. Chill. And I do mean chill.

Note: Cranberries remind people of Thanksgiving. That is such an incredibly wonderful time of year for most of us. How was your Thanksgiving last year? Remember when the police came to your house?

CURRIED (SIGH) CHICKEN (SIGH) SALAD

2 chicken breasts, cooked and cut into pieces
1 c. celery, chopped
1 c. green grapes
1/2 c. sliced green onions
1 tsp. salt
1/2 c. mayonnaise
1 to 2 tsp. curry powder, to taste
1/2 c. slivered almonds, toasted

(Sigh) Combine mayonnaise, salt and curry powder. (Sigh) Add to remaining ingredients. (Sigh) Chill. (Sigh) Serves 4 (Sigh) (Sigh) (Sigh) (Sigh) (Sigh) (Sigh) (Sigh) (Sigh)

HIS FIRST WIFE'S NAPA CABBAGE ORIENTAL SALAD

1 medium Napa cabbage
1 bunch green onions, sliced
1/2 c. slivered almonds
1 package ramen noodles, beef or chicken flavor
5 T. salad oil in all
2 T. sugar
2 T. cider vinegar
1 T. soy sauce
Flavor packet from ramen noodles

This might even be as good as the salad your husband's first wife made. In large bowl, whisk sugar, vinegar, soy sauce, 4 T. oil and flavor packet. Set aside. In large skillet over med. heat, brown crushed ramen noodles and almonds in 1 T. oil. He still thinks about her. Cool. Slice cabbage and add to dressing. Add green onions and toss. Let chill to blend flavors. Right before serving, stir in almond mixture, or add to each serving to keep its crunch. I wouldn't worry about it. Much. Serves 6 to 8

I HATE MY KIDS SOUTHWESTERN COBB SALAD

1 pkg. butter lettuce
1 can black beans, rinsed & drained
1/2 pint grape tomatoes
1 c. peeled & cubed jicama
1 avocado, sliced
3 c. frozen corn, thawed
1/3 c. black olives
Zesty ranch dressing or taco salad dressing

Layer lettuce on a large platter. Add vegetables in sections. Drizzle with dressing. Serves 6

Note: There's not much work to this one, which makes it perfect for those days when you feel totally drained by the children. Why do you suppose other mothers have so much energy? Do you really think that everybody's kids are as rotten as yours? Maybe you should have raised them instead of working at that loser job of yours.

Whatever is worth doing at all
Is worth doing well.

LOST AT SEA SHELL SALAD

8 oz crab or surimi
1/4 c. green onion, sliced
1/4 c. cucumber, chopped
1 hard-cooked egg, chopped

3/4 c. mayonnaise
1 T. lemon juice
2 tsp. dill weed
1/8 tsp. white pepper

Think about how no one cares about you as you combine the mayonnaise, lemon juice, dill weed and pepper. Fold in remaining ingredients. Do you feel lost? Just lost? This salad can be served in pita pockets, in tomato halves, avocado, pineapple, melon or papaya halves.

Note: My friend Steve thought he was lost at sea but when he woke up he had just wet the bed.

CRAZY MARY'S COLESLAW

1 bag coleslaw mix
1 c. mayonnaise
1 c. sugar

1/2 c. cider vinegar
Salt and pepper to taste

Whisk together dressing ingredients in large bowl. Add coleslaw and toss. Chill for a few hours before serving.

Note: Mary really is nuts and this really is her recipe. Believe it or not, she thinks this is hard to make. Of course, most of life is hard for her, from dawn to dusk. How about you? What have you done with your life that is worth talking about?

Let none escape, but try them all,
To boil or fry or bake.
We'll warrant they are just as good
As Mother used to make!

LARRY'S MARINATED VEGETABLE SALAD

2 cucumbers, sliced medium-thick
2 tomatoes, wedged
1 bunch green onions, sliced in 1/2 inch pieces
3 stalks celery, sliced medium thick
1 small can medium ripe olives
Italian dressing

Drizzle Italian dressing over vegetables, toss. Chill for several hours to marinate.

Note: The joke on the locked ward was that we could pour some Italian dressing over Larry and we would have a marinated vegetable. You had to be there.

JUST ME AND MY BROCCOLI SALAD

2 medium heads broccoli
6 oz. shredded cheddar
1 lb bacon, cooked and crumbled
1 c. sunflower seeds
1 medium. onion, diced
1 c. mayonnaise
1/2 c. sugar
3 T. vinegar

Did anyone like you in high school? Think about that question as you whisk together mayonnaise, sugar and vinegar. Combine all and chill. Chill. Were the other children cold to you? Why do you think that was? How come everybody liked your brother and not you?

MY LIFE HAS JUST WILTED LETTUCE SALAD

4 to 5 strips bacon
Lettuce for 4 servings
2 T. chopped green onions
3 T. bacon fat
1/4 c. wine vinegar
1 tsp. sugar
Salt and pepper to taste

Stare at yourself in a mirror for 20 minutes. Sad. Now cook bacon until crisp. Remove from pan and crumble. In drippings, stir in sugar and vinegar. Season with salt and pepper. Toss immediately with lettuce and garnish with reserved bacon. Serves 4

ARE U LUCKY 7 LAYER SALAD

6 celery stalks, chopped
1 c. cubed cheese
2 green peppers, chopped
1/2 to 1 onion, chopped
1 lg. package frozen peas, cooked and drained
1 head iceberg lettuce, chopped

Dressing:
1 c. sour cream
1 c. Miracle Whip
3 T. sugar

1 c. bacon bits
1 c. croutons
1 c. parmesan cheese

Layer first 6 ingredients in a bowl in order given. Mix sour cream, Miracle Whip and sugar. Spread over lettuce, making sure to seal edges. Just before serving, add bacon bits and mix salad. Top with croutons and parmesan cheese. Serves 12

Note: If you are not lucky, eating this salad will not do anything to change that. Some people are just not lucky. Lucky people meet the right girl or guy, have fun kids, win money and own neat boats. Do you?

AIRBORNE ORANGE CREAM FRUIT SALAD

1 20 oz. can pineapple tidbits, drained
1 16 oz. can peach slices, drained
1 11 oz. can mandarin oranges, drained
3 bananas, sliced
2 apples, cored & chopped, not peeled

1 (3 3/4 oz.) package instant vanilla pudding
1 1/2 c. milk
1/3 c. frozen orange juice, thawed, undiluted
3/4 c. sour cream

Combine fruit and set aside. Combine milk, pudding and orange juice. Beat until well blended. Beat in sour cream and pour over fruit. Chill.

Note: Never serve this to a room full of depressed people. The sunny color will enrage them and they will throw it at you.

Tomorrow is fresh, with no mistakes.

THE SALAD LOUISE MADE RIGHT BEFORE HER HUSBAND LEFT HER FOR A GUY

1 small head iceberg lettuce
1 can mandarin oranges, drained
1/3 c. celery, sliced
3 T. brown sugar
3 T. butter

1/3 c. slivered almonds
1/4 c. salad oil
2 T. vinegar
1/2 tsp. salt
Dash of red pepper sauce

In small saucepan over low heat, caramelize butter and brown sugar. Stir in almonds. Spoon onto waxed paper to cool. Break into small pieces. Shred lettuce and toss with oranges and celery. In blender, combine remaining ingredients and toss into lettuce. Sprinkle with candied almonds and serve. I sure hope your spouse comes home tonight; this is a good one and doesn't keep well.

SALAD NICOISE

1/4 c. olive oil
2 T. balsamic vinegar
1 T. Dijon mustard
1/2 tsp. salt
1/4 tsp. pepper
1/2 lb. small red potatoes or fingerling blend
1/2 lb. fresh green beans, trimmed

2 eggs, hard-boiled, quartered
2 6 oz. cans solid white tuna in water, drained
1/2 pint grape tomatoes
1/2 c. cucumber, peeled and thinly sliced
1/3 c. Nicoise or Kalamata olives
1 bag mixed greens

Whisk together first 5 ingredients. Set aside. In medium saucepan cook potatoes in enough water to cover until tender, about 5 to 10 minutes. Remove potatoes with a slotted spoon. Add green beans and cook until crisp-tender, about 2 minutes. Drain and rinse with cold water. Toss mixed greens with 2 T. dressing and place on platter. Arrange remaining vegetables in sections and drizzle with dressing. Serves 4

Note: Do you know how to say "Nicoise?" Who are you trying to impress? Canned tuna is not impressive, moron. You're supposed to use fresh tuna. And don't even think about using a can of those generic black olives that taste like cardboard. The whole thing about being impressive is that either you are or you aren't. And you ain't.

A GOOD CRY & THAI CHICKEN FETTUCCINI SALAD

6 oz. dried or 9 oz. fresh fettuccini, cooked, drained
3 chicken breast halves cooked, chopped
1/4 c. fresh cilantro, chopped
1/4 c. peanuts
1/4 c. thinly sliced red pepper strips

1 c. picante sauce
1/4 c. peanut butter
2 T. honey
2 T. orange juice
1 tsp. soy sauce
1/2 tsp. ground ginger

Have a good cry. Combine last 6 ingredients in saucepan and cook, stirring, over low heat until smooth. Sit on the floor and review your crummy life. Toss into remaining ingredients and chill to blend flavors. Cry. Cry. Cry. Cry. Cry. Serves 4 to 6

RECENTLY DECEASED CRANBERRY RELISH

12 oz bag of fresh cranberries
1 navel orange, washed, do not peel

3/4 c. sugar

In food processor, chop cranberries in batches, if necessary. Remove to medium bowl. Cut orange in half then into small sections. Process unpeeled orange pieces in batches, if necessary. Add to bowl and stir in sugar. Cover and chill.

Note: My friend Steve swore this made him feel healthier, younger and happier. Wrong. He would have been 49 next year.

SAFE GARLIC DRESSING

1 c. mayonnaise
3 T. milk
2 T. cider vinegar
1 clove garlic, crushed

1/2 tsp. sugar
1/4 tsp. salt
1/8 tsp. pepper

Blend all. Chill to blend flavors. Makes 1 cup

Note: You might as well eat this one. I mean it's not like anyone is going to want to kiss you. Do ya think?

BYE BYE PUPPY SPINACH SALAD DRESSING

2/3 c. safflower or other salad oil
1/4 c. cider vinegar
1/4 c. ketchup
3 T. honey
1 tsp. dark sesame oil
1 tsp. dry mustard
1/2 tsp. salt

Mix or shake all ingredients in a jar and place over heat until warm; do not boil. Toss into spinach salad. Makes 1 cup

Note: My mother made this salad the night my first puppy died so it always makes me cry. She makes it quite often.

SPICY PEANUT SALAD DRESSING

1/2 c. peanuts, toasted brown
1 garlic clove, crushed
2 scallions, sliced
1/2 tsp. toasted sesame oil
1 1/2 tsp. crushed red pepper
1/2 tsp. salt
1/3 c. rice wine vinegar
2/3 c. oil

Blend all in blender until peanuts are finely chopped. Think you can handle that? The hard part about being depressed is that you eventually realize it is all your fault. Something as simple as this dressing can seem insurmountable. It really isn't. It's just you. Snap out of it!

TOO MANY PEOPLE IN CHINA SALAD DRESSING

3/4 c. mayonnaise
5 T. rice vinegar
2 T. sugar
2 T. sesame oil
1 T. soy sauce
1/4 tsp. garlic powder

Mix all and chill to blend flavors. It's all just so sad. Think of all those people in China. At least some of them still have families that love them. I guess they are better off than you in most respects other than having fewer TV channels.

FIVE MINUTE THOUSAND ISLAND DRESSING

1/2 c. mayonnaise
3 T. ketchup
2 T. sweet pickle relish
1/2 tsp. minced dried onion

1/4 tsp. salt
1/4 tsp. pepper
1/4 tsp. caraway seeds

Combine and refrigerate. Well, that's done. Now what are you going to do for the rest of the day?

I FEEL LIKE GETTING PICKLED CUCUMBERS

1 c. vinegar
2 c. sugar
1 to 2 tsp. celery seed

7 c. sliced cucumber
2 onions, sliced
1/2 c. canning salt
Water to cover

In saucepan, combine vinegar, sugar and celery seed and bring to a boil. Cool and set aside. Combine remaining ingredients and let sit for 2 hours. Can you sit for two hours? Without crying? Or thinking about how he dumped you for another guy? Was it your shape? Your dull wit? Your bad legs? Your acne scars? Drain well and stir in dressing. Chill.

In cooking and in life as well
The only way that one can tell
What recipe is best, no doubt
Is read it through and try it out.

 # NOTES

Anorexic Tidbits

Vegetables & Side Dishes

SPANISH JUMPING JACK RICE

8 slices bacon, chopped
1 onion, chopped
16 oz. can diced tomatoes
1 c. uncooked rice

2 c. water or stock
1 T. chili powder
1 tsp. salt
1/8 tsp. pepper

Go weigh yourself. Sauté bacon, remove, drain and set aside. Mmmmm, smell that bacon! Go weigh yourself. Sauté onion in drippings until soft. Go weigh yourself. Add rice and cook 2 minutes. Add remaining ingredients, cover and simmer 45 minutes until rice is tender. Do 600 jumping jacks while rice is cooking. Stir in bacon and serve. Serves 1200.

NIGHTMARE THAI THUNDER THIGH FRIED RICE

1 1/2 pounds Hawaiian Chicken*
4 c. cold cooked rice (1 qt.)
1 fresh pineapple
1 red bell pepper, sliced
4 green onions, sliced
1 1/2 T. vegetable oil

3 to 5 cloves garlic, minced
2 T. sugar
2 T. Thai fish sauce (nam pla)
1 tsp. curry powder
Chopped fresh cilantro (or 1 tsp. dry)
Chopped peanuts, optional

Heat wok or large frying pan on high heat. Go weigh yourself. Add oil and garlic. Sauté until garlic is golden brown. Add red pepper and pineapple. Stir fry 2 minutes. Add rice and pat down. Cook 1 minute. Stir rice and pat down, cook 1 minute more. Add chicken, sugar, nam pla and curry powder and stir thoroughly, cooking 1 or 2 more minutes. Skip rope. Add green onion and heat through. Sprinkle with cilantro and chopped peanuts. Serves 400-600

HAWAIIAN CHICKEN RECIPE:

1/2 c. pineapple juice

1/3 c. soy sauce

Bring to boil in large frying pan. Add 1 1/2 pounds cut up chicken breast. Bring back to boil, cover, reduce heat and simmer 5 to 7 minutes until chicken is cooked through. Strain.

Note: That sure looks like a lot of food. Eat it all before you get up from the table. All of it. Every last bite! Now go weigh yourself.

28-MILE SWEET POTATOES WITH STREUSEL TOPPING

3 pounds sweet potatoes
2 eggs, beaten
1/4 c. butter, melted
1/2 c. milk or half & half
1/2 c. sugar
2 tsp. vanilla

1/4 tsp. salt
Topping
1/4 c. flour
1/4 c. softened butter
1/4 c. brown sugar
1 c. chopped pecans

Go weigh yourself. Run in place. Bake sweet potatoes at 350 for one hour or until tender. Cool, (can be baked ahead) peel and rice or mash into large bowl. Run faster. Combine remaining ingredients, pour into a 2-quart shallow baking dish. Do jumping jacks. Combine topping ingredients in small bowl and sprinkle on sweet potatoes. Skip rope. Bake one hour at 350, or 1 1/2 hours if baking with several other foods. Serve only on major holidays and invite plenty of guests so there are no leftovers!

ROASTED VEGETABLE REFLECTIONS

1 bag of new potatoes cut in half
1 bag of baby carrots
1 large onion cut in large chunks
1 or 2 red or green peppers cut in large chunks
Zucchini or yellow squash cut in large slices
Cherry or grape tomatoes

Asparagus spears
Brussels sprouts
About 2 T. olive oil
1 to 2 tsp. dried rosemary
1 tsp. minced garlic
Salt and pepper to taste

Look in mirror. Too chunky. Preheat oven to 425 degrees. Place potatoes, carrots, onions and peppers in one layer in large shallow roaster or jellyroll pan. Drizzle with olive oil and spices and mix to coat. Bake 10 to 20 minutes, and then stir. Add tomatoes and asparagus and stir in. Look in mirror some more and picture how these roasted vegetables will look plastered to your thighs. Bake another 10 to 20 minutes, or until vegetables are tender. Let cool and then wrap in newspaper and throw away. Pretend you are just "practicing" your cooking for when you really are hungry!

Our life is what our thoughts make it.

WAFFLE THIGHS FAVORITE THANKSGIVING DRESSING

1 box seasoned dressing
1 bag unseasoned dressing
2 c. celery,
1 c. onion, chopped

1/4 tsp. sage
1/4 tsp. salt
1 tsp. chicken bouillon
1 egg, slightly beaten

Your mom thinks you're too skinny. We don't. So go ahead and boil the onion and celery in water and butter called for on the box and bag of stuffing until tender. Add seasonings, stir in bread. Stir in egg and bake, covered at 350 for 1 hour, 1 1/2 hours with other foods. Bury a turkey neck in stuffing for extra flavor, remove before serving. Serves 80 or 90.

Note: Bake this in a disposable pan so you can leave any leftovers with the host. Holidays are so food-oriented. And you want to look nice in that new dress, don't you? Well, don't you, chubby?

CHEESY PUSHUPS & POTATOES

2 packages smoked sausage
1 large bag frozen hash browns
1 c. chopped onion (frozen, or sauté first)
1/2 c. chopped green pepper (opt.)
1 can cream of celery soup

1 pint half & half
3 oz cream cheese
1 tsp. salt
1 c. shredded cheddar cheese
1/2 stick butter, melted

Another high calorie, cholesterol-laden, high starch and fat recipe! Go back on that macrobiotic diet before it's too late. Or, do some pushups. Whip cream cheese with some half & half until smooth. Do some sit-ups. Combine all and spread in 8x12 greased pan. Do some jumping jacks. Bake at 350 for 1 hour, covered, then 30 minutes uncovered. May sprinkle with seasoned salt to add color. Look in mirror. Weigh yourself. Bon Appetit.

*Before you know what direction to take,
You have to know where you are going.*

CRAZY JANE'S TWO WAY POTATOES

2 lbs frozen hash browns
1 stick butter
1 pint sour cream
1 can cream of mushroom soup
3 c. shredded cheddar cheese
2 c. shredded Swiss cheese
2 c. corn flake crumbs
Salt and pepper to taste

Preheat oven to 350 degrees. Melt butter. Wow! Look at all that butter! Pour half in 9x13 cake pan. Mix the rest with crumbs and set aside. Put hash browns in 9 x 13 inch pan and season with salt and pepper. Sprinkle on Swiss cheese. Combine soup, sour cream and cheddar. Spread on top of Swiss layer. Sprinkle with crumbs and bake for 1 hour or more, until lightly browned and bubbly.

Note: My friend Jane is not only anorexic but a great cook—such a rare find! These are her favorites going down and coming back up. For an easier come-up, she recommends you double the sour cream.

MAMMOTH MARY'S SCALLOPED CORN

1 egg, beaten
1 c. cracker crumbs
1 c. milk
1 can creamed corn
1/4 c. onions
Salt and pepper to taste

Preheat oven to 350 degrees. Mix all ingredients and then pour into greased casserole and bake, uncovered, for 1 hour.

Note: Mary used to eat this quite often before she got control of her weight. Now she hardly touches it. Pity. But that's what can happen when you let your appetite get away from you. Care for a peanut? Oops! That's not an elephant! That's Mary! Silly!

Don't over look life's small joys
While searching for the big ones.

I DID TOO EAT RED CABBAGE

3 T. butter
1/2 c. onion, chopped
2 tart green apples, chopped
1/2 c. (or more) water
1/3 c. red currant jelly

1/4 c. cider vinegar
1 T. sugar
Dash nutmeg
Salt and pepper to taste
3 1/2 lb head red cabbage, shredded

Sauté onion in butter. Add remaining ingredients except cabbage. Simmer until jelly melts, stirring. Add cabbage, reduce heat to low and simmer, covered, about 45 minutes until cabbage is tender. Add more water, if needed.

Note: They can smell this one on your breath for days so maybe they'll back off bugging you to eat more.

SMELL MY GARLIC BREATH POTATOES

1 small bag new potatoes
1/2 stick butter, melted (about)

Garlic salt and pepper

Boil potatoes, with skins on, until just tender, about 15 minutes. Pinch your waist roll. Cool a bit and slice. Check your underarm flab in the mirror. Place potatoes in shallow casserole and brush with melted butter. Look over your shoulder and check out your butt. Sprinkle with garlic salt and pepper. Look in mirror. Broil 15 minutes until lightly browned while doing your yoga stretches.

Note: This is also an excellent recipe if people are bugging you about getting your weight up over that big, fat 79 lb. marker on your scale. They will definitely know you ate these babies!

To market, to market, to look for a roast;
Home again, home again, tuna on toast.

MY FAT GRANDMA'S SWEET POTATOES

2 large cans sweet potatoes
1 can pineapple chunks, juice reserved
4 T. butter

1/2 to 3/4 c. brown sugar
1/2 c. chopped pecans
About 1 c. mini marshmallows

Preheat oven to 350 degrees. Bring 1/4 c. pineapple juice, butter and brown sugar to a boil. Pour over potatoes layered in a greased casserole. Sprinkle with pecans. Bake 30 to 45 minutes, covered. Uncover and sprinkle with marshmallows. Bake 3 to 5 more minutes, until marshmallows are melted.

Note: In grandma's day you could be a big, fat cow and still find love. My, how times have changed!

OVEN FRIES FOR YOUR THIGHS

4 small potatoes, cut into fries
1 T. melted butter
1/4 c. parmesan

1/2 tsp. garlic salt
1/4 tsp. paprika
1/8 tsp. onion powder

Preheat oven to 400 degrees. Spread foil onto cookie sheet and spray with nonstick spray. Toss potatoes in butter, then in spices. Spread on cookie sheet and bake 25 to 30 minutes.

Note: These will quench your craving for fast-food French fries, which you haven't allowed past your lips for four years, three months and seven days. Enjoy them by yourself or share with all of your fat friends.

BUSY DAY ROASTED DIJON POTATOES

2 lb bag of new potatoes
2 T. olive oil
1 clove garlic, minced

1/2 tsp. Italian seasoning
1/3 c. Dijon mustard

Do seventy pushups. Preheat oven to 425 degrees. Stare at yourself in the mirror. Mix all but potatoes in small bowl. Weigh yourself. Cut larger potatoes in half and place all in 9x13 or other shallow pan. Run six miles. Toss with mustard mixture and bake 35 to 40 minutes, or until tender, stirring occasionally, while cleaning the house from top to bottom. Feel better now?

MOUNDS OF MUSTARD GREEN BEANS OR ASPARAGUS

1 lb fresh green beans or 1 bunch asparagus
2 T. butter
2 T. Dijon mustard
Salt and pepper to taste

How can anybody eat this much food? Think about that and then in a large frying pan, steam green beans or asparagus in about an inch of water, covered, until crisp-tender, about 3 to 5 minutes. Drain. Add butter and mustard and toss while heating through. Season and serve. And serve. And serve.

MASHED POTATOES TO MAKE AHEAD

5 lbs potatoes
1 stick butter
8 oz cream cheese
1/2 c. milk
2 eggs, beaten
Salt and pepper to taste

Just what I need, another potato recipe. Where are all the apple and celery stick recipes in this darn cookbook? Cook potatoes until tender. Drain and mash. Beat in remaining ingredients. Scoop into a greased casserole. When ready to bake, preheat oven to 350. Bake, covered, for 1 hour. If the whole idea of making these ahead of time bothers you, you might want to think what hell it is going to be when your parents make you eat EVERY SINGLE ONE OF THEM!

HIDDEN HORSERADISH POTATOES

1 lg. bag frozen hash browns
1 c. heavy cream
2 c. half & half
1/2 stick butter, melted
2 T. prepared horseradish
1/4 tsp. garlic powder
1/2 tsp. salt
1/4 tsp. pepper

Preheat oven to 350 degrees. Place hash browns in buttered casserole. Drizzle with melted butter. This is torture but you can do it, come on, come on! Combine remaining ingredients and pour over potatoes. Bake, uncovered, 45 to 60 minutes, until lightly browned and bubbling. This can also be made with thinly sliced potatoes and onions.

Note: Unlike a baked potato, these potatoes are easily hidden in your shoes.

NATIONAL MACARONI & CHEESE DAY

8 oz elbow mac, cooked & drained
8 oz shredded cheddar cheese
1 egg, beaten
2 c. evaporated milk
1 tsp. salt
2 T. butter

Preheat oven to 350 degrees. Layer half the macaroni, cheese, repeat. Combine egg, milk and salt and pour over macaroni. Dot with butter and bake 40 minutes. Serves a small nation if you cut each of the little elbow macaroni things into sixteen parts.

To lose your wealth is much.
To lose your health is more.
To lose your soul is such a loss,
that nothing can restore.
The world is such a busy place
There's so much hurry in it.
Isn't it nice sometimes
To pause for just a minute...

The Bulimic Buffet
Main Dishes

BIG BETTY'S BOMBASTIC BEAN CASSEROLE

1 lb. hamburger
3/4 lb. sliced bacon, diced
1 c. chopped onion
2 (31 oz.) cans pork & beans
16 oz. can kidney beans, drained
16 oz. can butter beans, drained

1 c. ketchup
1/2 c. brown sugar
1 tsp. liquid smoke
3 T. white vinegar
1 tsp. salt, and a dash of pepper

Brown hamburger and onion. Drain any grease. Brown bacon and drain. Combine all in crock pot. Cook on low 4 to 9 hours or in a 350 oven for 30 to 45 minutes. Serves 8 to 10, or 1 if you are really, really hungry. So, what else is new?

CUTE LIL' CONNIE'S CORNBREAD CASSEROLE

15 oz. can corn, drained
15 oz. can cream style corn
8.5 oz. package cornbread mix
1 egg

2 T. butter, melted
1 c. sour cream
2 c. shredded cheddar

Combine all ingredients. Pour in greased 11x7 baking dish. Bake at 400 for 25 to 30 minutes, until top and edges are golden brown.

Note: Our friend Connie eats like a hog and yet never seems to pack on the pounds. Must be her metabolism, don't you think?

VERY, VERY, VERY CREAMY SCALLOPED POTATOES CASSEROLE

6 medium potatoes, sliced
4 T. butter
4 T. flour
2 1/2 c. milk
1/2 tsp. salt (or to taste)

1/4 tsp. paprika
1/4 tsp. dried mustard
Dash of garlic powder
1/2 c. onion, chopped
6 T. butter

You are getting very hungry. Relax and listen to my voice. You are very, very, very hungry. Preheat oven to 350 degrees. Make white sauce with butter, flour and milk. Boil one minute. Season with spices. Set aside. In a 2 quart buttered casserole, layer half the potatoes and onions, half the sauce and repeat. Dot with butter. Cover and bake 30 minutes. Uncover and bake 60 - 70 minutes until potatoes are tender. Stare at it for hours, sweating, before giving in and eating it. Serves 8

200 LB. MACARONI & CHEESE CASSEROLE

7 oz. elbow macaroni
8 oz. processed cheese, cut into chunks
2/3 c. milk

3 T. butter
1/4 tsp. salt
Pepper to taste

Cook macaroni for 6 minutes and then drain. Do 75 sit-ups. Place in 9x9 greased casserole dish. In large micro-safe bowl, melt cheese with milk and butter. Add salt and pepper and pour over macaroni. Bake at 350, uncovered, for 30 minutes. Serves 6-8

Note: We call this one 200 lb. Macaroni & Cheese Casserole because that is what you will look like if you eat stuff like this all of the time.

PORKY PENNY'S GREAT GOULASH CASSEROLE

7 oz. elbow macaroni
1 lb. hamburger
1/2 c. each: onion and celery, diced
1 can tomato soup
8 oz. can tomato sauce
16 oz. can diced tomatoes, undrained

1 tsp. salt
1/4 tsp. pepper
1/2 tsp. sugar
1 tsp. chili powder
1/8 tsp. garlic powder

Cook macaroni six minutes and drain. Brown hamburger, onion and celery in a large pan. Drain any grease. That skirt sure looks tight. Oh, those are shorts? Sad. Mix in all ingredients and bake, covered, at 350 degrees for 30 to 45 minutes. Can serve up to 8, but hey, who's counting?

CHUNKS AND CHUNKS OF HAMBURGER HOT DISH

1 bag small red or yellow potatoes
1 bag baby carrots
1 onion, diced
1 lb hamburger
1 can cream of celery or mushroom soup

1/2 soup-can milk
3/4 tsp. salt
Pepper to taste
Optional: 1 c. shredded cheddar

Brown hamburger and onion. Cut potatoes in half and carrots into large chunks. Oops. Did we say "chunks" again? Combine all and bake, covered, at 350 degrees for 1 1/2 hours. Optional: Sprinkle cheddar on the last 5 minutes. Serves 8

PORKY PATTI'S POLISH REUBEN CASSEROLE

4 oz. medium egg noodles, cooked and drained
1 lb smoked sausage, sliced
1 can mushroom soup
1/2 soup-can milk
1/4 c. chopped onion
1 T. Dijon mustard
1 c. shredded Swiss cheese
16 oz. can sauerkraut, drained
1 to 2 T. melted butter
2/3 c. rye bread or cracker crumbs

Sauté onions in a little butter until soft. Stir in soup, milk and mustard. In buttered 9" casserole, spread sauerkraut. Layer on noodles. Spoon soup mixture over noodles and sprinkle with cheese. Top with sausage slices. Mix melted butter with crumbs and sprinkle over. Bake, uncovered, at 350 degrees for 30 to 45 minutes, until bubbling. Serves 4 to 6 unless you eat like Patti!

Note: Creamy goin' down. Explosive comin' up!

COLORFUL POTATO, HAM & SPINACH CASSEROLE

20 oz. package frozen hash browns
6 oz. ham, cubed
10 oz. frozen spinach, thawed and well-drained
1 can celery soup
1 c. sour cream
1/8 tsp. nutmeg
Salt and pepper to taste
8 oz. shredded cheddar cheese

Preheat oven to 350 degrees. In saucepan, heat spinach, soup, sour cream, nutmeg and salt and pepper to taste. Fold in ham and potatoes and place in greased 9x13 pan. Sprinkle with cheese. Bake 45 to 50 minutes. Easy going down, pretty coming up!

LINDA'S SAUSAGE AND WILD RICE CASSEROLE

1 c. wild rice
1 lb. bulk pork sausage
2 (3 oz.) cans sliced mushrooms
1 can cream of mushroom soup
1 medium onion, sliced thin
Salt and pepper to taste

Stand in front of the mirror for five minutes. Do you like what you see? Any room for improvement? Cook rice until tender and set aside. Brown sausage, drain. Stir in mushrooms and soup. Add to rice and season with salt and pepper. Stand in front of the mirror for another five minutes. Did you get a little bigger? Put half the rice mixture in a buttered casserole. Top with sliced onion. Add remaining rice mixture. Stand in front of the mirror for five minutes. Yup. You did get bigger! Bake, covered, at 350 degrees for 60 minutes. Serves 8 normal people or one oinker like Linda.

BOY I'M STUFFED CABBAGE

1 head cabbage
1 1/2 lbs. hamburger
1/2 c. uncooked rice
1 small onion, diced fine
1 egg, beaten
1 tsp. salt
1/4 tsp. pepper

Sauce:
8 oz. can tomato sauce
28 oz. can diced tomatoes (or 2 16 oz. cans)
1 tsp. salt
1/4 tsp. pepper

Core cabbage. Microwave until outer leaves are soft. Trim off hard ribs. Use 12 leaves. Combine meat, rice, onion, egg, salt and pepper. Mound on each leaf, fold sides over and roll up. Place seam side down in Dutch oven. Pour sauce ingredients over. Cover and simmer on low heat 1 hour. Eat some. Eat some more. Now eat some more. Now eat some more. Now eat some more. Now eat some more. Now eat some more. Now eat some more.

PORTABLE STUFFED GREEN PEPPERS

4 green peppers
1 lb hamburger
1/2 onion, diced
1 c. cooked rice

1 tsp. salt
15 oz. can tomato sauce
16 oz. can diced tomatoes

Preheat oven to 350 degrees. Hollow out peppers, microwave in covered dish with a little water 6 to 8 minutes until crisp-tender. Brown hamburger and onion, drain. Add rice and season. Spoon into peppers. Combine sauce and pour over peppers. Bake, uncovered 30 to 40 minutes. Serves 1 hungry camper!

Note: These stuffed green peppers can also be carried in your purse for those emergency hunger pangs. They also make a great weapon.

PURGING DOWN AT THE OKAY CORRAL CHILI

1 lb hamburger or 2 lb. chuck roast, chopped coarse
1/2 c. chopped onion
16 oz. can red beans
16 oz. can refried beans
8 oz. tomato sauce

1 c. water
1 tsp. chopped hot red peppers
Cayenne pepper to taste
1/2 tsp. salt
3 T. chili powder
1 T. molasses

Brown beef and onions. Add remaining ingredients. Cover and simmer 1 hour. Serves 6. Again and again and again. Saddle up, pardner.

ALMOST INSTANT GRATIFICATION
BEEF GOULASH STEW

1 lb hamburger	1/2 c. water
1/2 c. chopped onion	1 tsp. Worcestershire sauce
10 1/4 oz. can beef gravy	10 oz. package frozen peas & carrots
7 1/2 oz. can tomatoes	1 c. uncooked fine noodles

In Dutch oven, brown beef and onions. Stir in gravy, tomatoes, water and Worcestershire. Bring to boil. Add peas and carrots and noodles. Return to boil. Cover and simmer 10 minutes. Serves 4. Gee, that was quick, wasn't it? Dig in!

CHICKEN & DUMPLINGS

2 chicken breasts	3/4 c. water & 4 heaping spoons cornstarch
1 c. each: chopped onion, carrot, and celery	
4 to 6 c. chicken stock	Dumplings:
1 tsp. salt	2 c. baking mix
1/2 tsp. white pepper	2/3 c. milk or more
1 T. tarragon	

Sauté vegetables. Add broth and simmer chicken breasts 20 minutes. Remove breasts and dice and place back in broth. Add seasonings. Stir together dumplings and drop 10 or 12 onto broth. Cook 10 minutes uncovered. Cover and cook 10 minutes more. Serves 6

Note: There is something about a great big bucket of chicken and dumplings that is just too much for words! Hide a bucket in your "secret section" of the garage refrigerator.

OUT OF CONTROL OVEN BARBEQUE

4 to 6 lb. boneless chuck	1 1/4 c. barbeque sauce
1 can cream of mushroom soup	1 package onion soup mix

You can handle it, sure. Just eat a little and then stop. Sure you will. Yeah. Right. In roaster, cover meat with soup. Pour barbeque sauce over soup. Sprinkle with dry soup mix. Cover roast and bake at 350 degrees for 3+ hours for shredded beef. Drain off fat and shred meat. Dive in. Serves 8, or one extra-hungry debutant.

HIDDEN HAM LOAF

1 1/2 to 2 lbs. leftover ham (Bet you got lots of that!)
1/2 c. dry breadcrumbs
1 egg
1/2 c. milk
Maple syrup

Preheat oven to 350 degrees. Cut ham into chunks and process until coarsely ground. Combine ham, breadcrumbs, eggs and milk. Scoop into greased loaf pan. Drizzle maple syrup over the top and bake for 30 minutes. This dish can be prepared ahead and hidden in the clothes hamper. Good warm or cold.

BARB'S BAKED PORK TENDERLOIN

1 whole pork tenderloin
1/4 c. Dijon mustard
1/4 c. red currant jelly

Preheat oven to 325 degrees. Place meat in shallow roaster. Mix jelly and mustard, spread on meat and bake for 40-45 minutes.

Note: My friend Steve called Barb a Porker and she broke his nose. I always think of her when I eat this dish or see a cement truck.

BAKED PORK CHOPS IN MYSTERY MUSHROOM GRAVY

4 to 6 pork chops
1/2 c. chopped onion
1 can mushroom soup
3/4 soup-can milk
Few dashes Worcestershire sauce
1/8 tsp. salt
Dash pepper

In large frying pan, brown pork chops and place in greased casserole (not too shallow). Brown onions. Add soup, milk and seasonings and bring to a boil. Pour over pork chops. Bake, covered, at 350 degrees for about 2 hours until meat is very tender. Can also be cooked in crock-pot on high. Serves 4

Note: Who do you think invented gravy? What size do you think she wore?

DISAPPEARING MEAT LOAF

1 1/2 lbs hamburger
1 chopped onion
1 egg
1/2 c. dry breadcrumbs
1/2 c. tomato juice or vegetable juice
3/4 tsp. salt
1/8 tsp. pepper
2 T. horseradish
1 T. Worcestershire sauce
1/8 tsp. garlic powder
3 or 4 strips of bacon for top

Combine all ingredients and put into greased loaf pan. Lay bacon strips over top. Bake at 350 degrees for 1 1/2 hours. Gee, that whole meat loaf was in the fridge when your boyfriend went to work this morning. Oh where, oh where can it be?

FANTASY HAMBURGERS IN SAUCE

1 lb. ground sirloin
2 T. butter
1 tsp. Worcestershire sauce
1/4 tsp. lemon juice
1 onion, sliced
1 c. mushrooms, sliced (or 1/2 c. canned)
Dash of garlic powder

Make 4 patties, set aside. Look at pictures of slim fashion models. Melt butter in frying pan and add all other ingredients While frying, look at more pictures of slim fashion models. Sauté 2 minutes over medium heat and push to edges of pan. Look at lots more pictures of slim fashion models. Add patties and cook until done. Tear up pictures of slim fashion models. Ain't going to happen. Season with salt and pepper. Makes 4

CHICKEN PIE BINGE

2 c. cooked chicken pieces
1/2 bag frozen peas & carrots or mixed vegetables
1/2 c. chopped onion
1 can cream of celery soup
1/2 soup-can milk
1 tsp. paprika
Salt and pepper to taste
Pastry for 1 crust pie

Preheat oven to 375 degrees. Microwave peas and carrots for 4 minutes in 1 T. water. Drain. Place chicken and peas and carrots in pie plate. Sauté onion until tender. Stir in soup and milk and heat to boiling. Add seasonings. Pour over chicken mixture. Place pastry over and crimp. Cut out a small circle in the middle or slit crust a few times. Bake for 45 minutes until crust is golden. Let cool 10 minutes before slicing. Serves 6

Note: This is one great pie. You might want to make several at a time. Just to be safe. And while you are at it, add a bottom crust, too. Go for it!

THE LOCKED WARD'S FAVORITE FRIED CHICKEN

1 fryer chicken, cut up
About 1 c. milk
1 c. flour
1/2 tsp. baking powder

1 tsp. salt
1 tsp. paprika
1/2 tsp. pepper
1/8 tsp. garlic salt

Soak chicken in salt water 30 minutes or up to 12 hours. Rinse and drain, pat dry. Combine dry ingredients in shallow bowl. Dip chicken pieces in milk, then roll in flour mixture. Place pieces on cookie sheet and let chill for 30 minutes. In electric frying pan, on high, brown pieces, in batches if necessary, in about 1/4 inch of oil. Return all chicken to pan, reduce heat to med low, cover and cook 45 minutes. Turn pieces occasionally. Take lid off and let cook 10 more minutes or so until crispy.

Note: Mark tried to put a thigh in Betty's feeding tube. Don't even think about it.

OVEN BAKED AND YOU GET TO WHACK IT CHICKEN KIEV

4 chicken breast halves
1/4 c. softened butter
1/2 tsp. tarragon, crumbled
1/2 c. flour

2 eggs, beaten
1 c. dry breadcrumbs
Melted butter

Preheat oven to 425 degrees. Lightly grease an 8" square baking dish. Pound chicken until uniformly thin. Just a little more. Just a little more. Really whack that thing now. Just a little more. Wow. Bet you lost a pound doing all of that whacking. Hey, let's whack some more. Whack! Good. Now stir tarragon into butter and spoon equal portions in center of chicken pieces. Roll up and secure with toothpicks. Dip in flour, egg, and then bread crumbs. Bake until golden brown, about 20 to 25 minutes, basting several times with melted butter, if desired. Serves 4

It is great to grow old if one keeps young in doing so.

BIG FAT FISH IN FOIL

2 Orange Roughie fillets　　　　　　　2 T. butter
1 bunch green onions, sliced

Preheat oven to 375 degrees. Spray large piece of heavy-duty foil with cooking spray. Place one fillet in center. Put half the butter and onions on fillet and season with salt and pepper. Fold up into a package, sealing tight. Repeat with remaining filet. Bake on cookie sheet for about 20 minutes. Can also be cooked on grill. Serves 2

Note: Actually this is a bad title. Fish aren't big and fat. But I guess if you ate enough of them you would become big and fat. Or bigger and fatter as the case may be.

HOLY GRAIL SEAFOOD LASAGNA

1/2 lb. lasagna noodles, cooked　　　　Salt & pepper to taste
2 c. cottage cheese　　　　　　　　　　2 cans cream of shrimp soup
8 oz package cream cheese, softened　 1 1/2 lbs crab meat, picked over
1 c. chopped green onions　　　　　　　3/4 lb small cooked shrimp
1 egg, beaten　　　　　　　　　　　　　 1 c. grated sharp cheddar cheese
1 tsp. dried basil　　　　　　　　　　　 1 c. grated mozzarella cheese

Preheat oven to 350 degrees. Combine cottage cheese, cream cheese, onion, egg, basil salt & pepper, soup, crab and shrimp. Line a greased 9x13 pan with half the noodles. Top with half the seafood mixture. Repeat. Bake for 15 minutes. Top with grated cheeses and bake 45 minutes longer. Let stand 15 minutes before cutting into squares. Serves 12

Note: This puppy is the holy grail of overeating. Enjoy!

GO AHEAD AND MAKE MY BURGER

1 1/2 lb ground chuck (sorry chuck)　　2 tsp. yellow mustard
1 c. Swiss cheese, grated　　　　　　　Salt & pepper to taste
1/2 c. chopped black olives　　　　　　6 hamburger buns

Quit focusing so much on food. Brown beef and onion, season with salt and pepper; drain. Quit it. Mix in mustard and olives, heat. Quit it. And don't taste. Grate the Swiss cheese and stir in until melted. Quit it. Quit it. Quit it. Quit it. Fill hamburger buns and wrap each in foil and bake at 350 degrees for 20 minutes. Quit it. Cool 5 minutes and serve. Quit it. Serves 4 to 6

LOST CAUSE CASSEROLE

1 bag coleslaw mix
1 medium onion, diced
1/2 lb. hamburger
3/4 tsp. salt

1/8 tsp. pepper
1/8 tsp. garlic powder
1 can tomato soup

Brown hamburger and onion in large frying pan. Drain any grease. Add coleslaw mix, seasonings, and gently stir in tomato soup. Cover and cook on low for 30 minutes, stirring occasionally, until cabbage is very tender, or can be baked at 350 degrees, covered, for one hour. Serves 6 to 8

Note: This one is so good your diet can wait until tomorrow. Go ahead. It's not like anybody will ever know but you and the dog. Oh, you ate her? Sad.

POTATO & HAMBURGER CASSEROLE WITH MANY HAPPY RETURNS

4 to 5 medium potatoes, sliced
1 onion, diced
1 lb hamburger

1 large can vegetable beef soup
1/4 can water

Lock yourself in the bathroom. Come out. Brown hamburger, combine all in a 2-quart casserole and bake at 350 degrees for 1 to 1 1/2 hours. Lock yourself in the bathroom. Come out. Stir once or twice. Lock yourself in the bathroom. Come out. Enjoy. Again. And again. And again.

QUICKIE QUICHE

3/4 to 1 lb. ham or sausage
1/2 c. onion, thinly sliced
1 1/2 c. sharp cheddar, grated
1 T. flour
3 eggs, beaten
16 oz. can evaporated milk (or half & half)

1 T. parsley flakes
3/4 tsp. seasoned salt
1/4 tsp. pepper
1 pie crust

Preheat oven to 350 degrees. Brown meat and onion. Drain. Combine cheese and flour. Spread meat in pie crust and top with cheese. Mix remaining ingredients and pour into pie shell. Bake on cookie sheet 35 to 40 minutes, or until browned and set.

Note: You never know when you are going to need a quick quiche. Keep several handy in the freezer for after your husband goes to work.

GUILTLESS SLOPPY JOES

1 lb. lean ground beef
1/2 c. barbeque sauce
1/2 c. ketchup
1 T. mustard
2 T. brown sugar

2 T. cider vinegar
Splash Worcestershire sauce
1/2 capful liquid smoke
1/4 c. water
1/2 tsp. salt and pepper to taste

Brown ground beef and drain. Add remaining ingredients and simmer, covered, for 20 to 30 minutes. If mixture gets too dry, add a little more water. Serves 6 to 8 or one hungry person. Go ahead. You won't feel that guilty. Eat the whole darn pot of them. Yum. Hey, next time why not double the recipe?

ALMOST OVERNIGHT EGG CASSEROLE

8 slices bread, crusts removed and cubed
2 c. milk
8 eggs, beaten
1 tsp. salt

1 tsp. dry mustard
1/8 tsp. pepper
2 c. grated cheddar cheese
1 c. cubed ham

Butter an 8x8x2 glass dish. In a medium bowl, whisk eggs, milk and seasonings. Gently stir in bread, cheese and ham. Pour into casserole, cover and refrigerate at least 4 hours or overnight. Think you can wait that long? Yeah, right. Bake at 325 degrees for 1 hour. Cool 10 minutes before serving. Serves 9

SIZE SIX SESAME NOODLES WITH PEANUT SAUCE

1 lb vermicelli or angel hair pasta
3 T. dark sesame oil, in all
3 large garlic cloves
4 green onions, minced fine
1 inch ginger root, chopped fine
1/3 c. peanut butter

1/4 c. soy sauce
1/4 c. chicken broth
1 T. rice vinegar
1 T. oil
2 tsp. sugar
1 tsp. crushed red pepper

Cook pasta according to package directions, drain and toss with 2 T. dark sesame oil. Set aside. In processor, add 1 tablespoon sesame oil and remaining ingredients and process until mixed. Toss over pasta and chill. Can be garnished with julienned cucumber. Serves 6 to 8.

Note: We called this one Size Six Sesame Noodles with Peanut Sauce just to make you feel good. It's as close as you'll ever get to a size six.

NOTES

Rising Addictions
Breads & Rolls

PETE'S OVER-THE-COUNTER POPOVERS

5 eggs	2 c. flour
2 c. milk	1 tsp. salt

Preheat oven to 450 degrees. Grease popover pans. Beat eggs slightly. Add milk, flour and salt. Beat just until smooth but do not overbeat. Fill pans 1/2 to 2/3 full. Bake 25 minutes. While you are waiting, count the number of days until you can refill your prescriptions. That long, huh? Lower oven temperature to 350 degrees and bake 10 to 20 minutes more, until deep golden brown. Makes 12

Note: These popovers are a favorite, and my friend Pete thinks they are so good they should require a prescription!

BUTTERSCOTCH DROP SOBER SCONES

2 c. flour	1/2 c. chilled butter, diced
1/3 c. packed brown sugar	1 c. butterscotch chips (6 oz.)
1 T. baking powder	1/2 c. (or more) chilled heavy cream
1/4 tsp. salt	1 large egg

Don't drink today. Just heat the oven to 400 degrees. Sift dry ingredients into medium bowl. Cut in butter until coarse meal forms. Mix in butterscotch chips. Did that make you thirsty for a big tumbler full of the real thing? Don't drink today. Whisk cream and egg together and add gradually to dry ingredients, tossing with fork until dough comes together in moist clumps. Add more cream by teaspoons if too dry. Drop by 1/4 cupfuls onto cookie sheet. Bake until golden brown and toothpick inserted in center comes out clean, about 20 minutes. Don't drink today. Eat all of them while still warm. Feel better? Didn't think so.

When all is said and done,
More is said than done.

WHITE CHOCOLATE RASPBERRY SCONES

2 c. flour
1/3 c. sugar
1 T. baking powder
1/4 tsp. salt
1/2 c. chilled butter, diced

1/2 bag white chocolate chips (6 oz.)
1/2 bag frozen raspberries, slightly thawed
1 egg
1/2 c. cream or half & half

Preheat oven to 400 degrees. Sift dry ingredients together. A little shaky today? Cut in butter until coarse meal forms. Gently stir in raspberries and chips. Whisk together egg and cream and gradually add to dry ingredients, tossing with fork until dough forms moist clumps. Add more cream if dough is too dry. Hey, how much did you drink last night? Drop by 1/4 cupfuls onto an air bake cookie sheet. Bake about 20 minutes, or until golden brown and toothpick comes out clean. Better wait till noon for your first drink today. I think your boss knows. Try an air-bake sheet to avoid burning chips. Makes 14

QUICK SCORE SCONES

2 c. flour
1/4 c. sugar
1 T. baking powder

1/4 to 1/2 tsp. salt
1 2/3 c. heavy cream

Got a scone jones? Preheat oven to 450 degrees. Grease cookie sheet. In large bowl, mix flour, baking powder and salt. Stir in cream, enough so dough leaves sides of bowl and forms a ball. Drop dough by 1/4 cupfuls 1 inch apart on cookie sheet. Brush with cream and sprinkle with sugar. Bake 12 to 15 minutes until light golden brown. Immediately remove from cookie sheet. Serves 12

MORNING AFTER CHEESE BISCUITS

2 c. flour
1 T. baking powder
1/4 tsp. salt

1/4 c. butter, chilled
1 c. shredded cheese or cheese blend
2/3 c. milk

Just stop shaking. In large bowl stir together dry ingredients. Stop shaking. Cut in butter until coarse crumbs form. Clasp hands together. Stir in cheese. Make a well in center and add milk. Using a fork, stir just until moistened. Stop shaking. Turn dough out onto floured surface. Knead 10 to 12 times or until dough holds together. Stop shaking. Pat lightly to a half-inch thickness. Using a 1 1/2 inch biscuit cutter. cut into rounds. Place 1 inch apart on ungreased cookie sheet. Bake at 450 degrees for 10 to 12 minutes or until bottoms are golden brown. Serve with tomato juice but do NOT put anything in it. Well, okay, just a little one to open your eyes.

GARLIC BREATH PULL-APARTS

1 package of 8 biscuits, original style
3/4 stick butter
2 cloves garlic, minced
1 to 2 tsp. Italian seasoning (optional)

Melt butter in small, oven-proof omelet pan. Add garlic and seasoning. Cut biscuits into fourths and roll around in butter, covering every speck. Place pan in 350 degree oven for 20 to 25 minutes. Serves 8

Note: These ought to cover up anything else on your breath. Perfect for before church.

STUFFED MAGIC MUSHROOM BREAD

1 loaf Vienna or French bread
8 oz (2 c.) shredded Swiss cheese
1 pint chopped fresh mushrooms
1/2 c. chopped green onions
1/2 c. butter
2 tsp. lemon juice
2 T. poppy seeds
2 tsp. Dijon mustard

Combine cheese, mushrooms and onions. Do you feel anything yet? Stuff into almost sliced through Vienna bread or spoon on top of French bread sliced in half lengthwise. Do you feel anything yet? Melt butter and stir in remaining ingredients Drizzle over mushroom mixture. Wrap loosely in foil and place on cookie sheet and bake at 350 degrees for about 45 minutes. Do you feel anything yet? Can also be made on a grill. Serves 12

THROWING MUFFINS

1 c. flour
2 T. sugar
1 tsp. baking powder
1/2 tsp. salt
1/4 c. plus 2 T. milk
2 T. oil or melted butter
1 egg
1 package (10 oz) frozen chopped spinach, thawed and squeezed dry
4 oz. shredded cheddar cheese

Preheat oven to 350 degrees. Grease 6 muffin cups. In a large bowl combine dry ingredients Add milk, oil and eggs. Stir with wooden spoon just until combined. Stir in spinach and cheese. Bake 20 to 25 minutes until wooden pick inserted in center comes out clean. Serves 6

Note: Eddy named these throwing muffins. They should not be consumed with alcohol. They no longer serve these on the detox ward.

OUR DETOX UNIT'S FAVORITE BISCUITS

1/2 c. shredded cheddar cheese
2 c. biscuit baking mix
2/3 c. milk

1/4 c. melted butter
1/2 tsp. garlic powder

Preheat oven to 450 degrees. Combine first 3 ingredients with wooden spoon until soft dough forms. Beat vigorously 30 seconds. Drop spoonfuls onto ungreased cookie sheet. Bake 8 to 10 minutes. Brush butter mixed with garlic powder over warm biscuits. Serves 8 to 10

Note: What kind of fool would serve biscuits in a detox unit and expect things to remain calm?

CHEESE & GARLIC BREATH BISCUITS

2 c. flour
2 tsp. baking powder
1 tsp. salt
4 T. butter, chilled

1 c. shredded cheddar
1 c. milk
Melted butter
Garlic salt

Preheat oven to 450 degrees. In large bowl, mix dry ingredients. Cut in butter until crumbly. Quickly stir in cheese and milk until just blended. Drop by tablespoonfuls onto greased cookie sheet. Brush with melted butter. Sprinkle with garlic salt. Bake 12 to 15 minutes. Serves 12

Note: Feeling kind of rancid today? Are your pores oozing stale booze? Need a camouflage smell to get through the day? These are perfect!

*Life is what happens to you while
You are making other plans.*

NOT AS FUN STICKY BUNS

2 tubes refrigerated biscuits
4 T. sugar
1 tsp. cinnamon
1/2 c. brown sugar
1/2 c. butter or margarine
1/4 c. light corn syrup

Preheat oven to 350 degrees. Bring brown sugar, butter and corn syrup to a boil in medium saucepan and set aside. Cut biscuits in quarters. Combine sugar and cinnamon in a small bowl and coat each piece of dough. Place half the dough in a shallow baking pan and pour half the syrup over. Repeat with remaining. Bake 30 minutes. Let cool 3 to 5 minutes and turn out onto foil. (Oven to 325 degrees if using a bundt pan)

Note: The nurses think these are great because they cannot be thrown as easily as the previous recipes. And if you do get hit with one, it is much hard to throw back because it sticks to your hand.

PEPPER CHEESE BEER BREAD

2 c. flour
5 oz. shredded pepper-jack cheese
1 tsp. sugar
3/4 tsp. baking powder
1/2 tsp. baking soda
1/2 tsp. salt
1/3 c. melted butter
1 c. beer (8 oz) plus two or three
  cases held in reserve
2 eggs, slightly beaten

Hide your car keys. Preheat oven to 350 degrees. In large bowl, mix dry ingredients and 1 cup of cheese. Stir in butter, beer and eggs just until moistened. Spoon into a 9x5 greased loaf pan. Sprinkle with remaining cheese. Bake 45 to 55 minutes or until a wooden pick inserted in center comes out clean. Remove from pan and cool 10 minutes before serving. Makes 1 loaf.

Note: It takes my friend Steve 2 cases of beer to make one loaf of this bread. I just don't understand.

ONE WAFFLE AT A TIME CORN BREAD

1 package corn muffin mix
**An equal amount of milk to make a
  fairly thick batter**

Preheat and oil an 8-inch waffle iron. Pour a scant cup of batter onto iron.

Note: Not real complicated and that's what makes this recipe special for days on which you have court appearances. Keep it simple. One waffle at a time.

DANISH HUFF & PUFF NOSE PASTRIES

1 c. flour
1/2 c. butter
2 T. water
1/2 c. butter
1 c. water
1 tsp. almond extract
1 c. flour

3 eggs

1 T. melted butter
2 T. cream
1 c. powdered sugar
1/4 tsp. vanilla

Preheat oven to 350 degrees. Mix first 3 ingredients into pastry. Pat into two strips, 12 x 3 inches, 3 inches apart on an ungreased cookie sheet. Bring next two ingredients to a boil, take off heat and add almond extract and flour. Stir quickly to prevent lumping. Add eggs, one at a time, beating well each time. Spread over pastry strips and bake for 45 to 60 minutes until light brown and crisp. While baking, mix together last 4 ingredients into frosting. Watch that powdered sugar. Now, what does that remind you of? Spread onto puff immediately after baking. Sprinkle puff with chopped nuts, if desired.

Note: Don't play with the powdered sugar. We'd hate to reawaken your sleeping demons.

NOSE WATERING BELGIAN WAFFLES

4 eggs, separated
1 tsp. sugar
1/2 tsp. salt
1 c. milk

1/2 tsp. vanilla
4 T. butter, melted and cooled
1 c. flour
NO powdered sugar for garnish

Beat egg whites until just stiff and set aside. In a medium bowl, beat yolks, sugar and salt until thick and fluffy. Blend in milk, vanilla and butter. Gradually add flour and blend well. Fold in egg whites. Spoon onto preheated waffle iron and bake. Makes 5 five-inch square waffles.

Note: I knew a guy in L.A. that got so excited by all of the powdered sugar on top of one of these puppies that he tried to snort it. We were asked to leave the restaurant and his HMO refused to pick up the tab for having the waffle removed from his nose. That is why we leave the powdered sugar out of our recipe. Ugly is as ugly does.

Schizophrenic Fare
Cakes, Cookies & Just Desserts

THE GOVERNMENT'S SECRET CHOCOLATE TRUFFLE COOKIES

1 1/4 c. butter, softened
2 1/4 c. powdered sugar
1/3 c. cocoa powder
1/4 c. sour cream
1 T. vanilla
2 1/4 c. flour
Pinch of salt
2 c. (12 oz) semi-sweet chocolate chips
1/4 c. chocolate sprinkles

Take out a four-foot section of heavy-duty foil and fashion it into a helmet. Place on head, covering your ears. Put on mirrored sunglasses. Lock the doors. Take this recipe out of your hiding place. In large mixing bowl, cream butter, sugar and cocoa until light and fluffy. Beat in sour cream and vanilla. Add flour and pinch of salt and mix well. Shhhhhhhhhhh. They can hear you right through the walls. Stir in chocolate chips. Refrigerate 1 hour. Roll into 1 inch balls and dip into chocolate sprinkles. Place 2 inches apart on ungreased cookie sheet. Bake at 325 degrees for 10 minutes or until set. Cool 5 minutes before removing to wire rack. Makes 5 1/2 dozen, if you live long enough to enjoy them.

OUR FAVORITE COFFEE CAKE

1 box yellow cake mix
1 small instant butterscotch pudding mix
1 small instant vanilla pudding mix
1 c. oil
1 c. water
4 eggs

Topping
1 c. brown sugar
1 c. chopped nuts
1 T. cinnamon

In large mixing bowl, combine cake mix, pudding mixes, oil, water and eggs. Hey, who did that? Beat on medium speed for two minutes. Hey, how did I get here? Mix topping ingredients together and fold half into the batter. Pour batter into a greased 9x13 cake pan. Walk in circles around the kitchen. Sprinkle with remaining topping. Bake at 350 degrees for 35-45 minutes, or until done. Hey! Why did my wife come and bake me a cake? Is it visiting day? Is it my birthday?

DONNA'S ANTI-MIND-READING CAKE

1/2 c. soft butter
1/2 c. sugar
2 eggs
1 c. flour

1/2 tsp. baking powder
1/2 tsp. vanilla
Pinch of salt

Preheat oven to 350 degrees. Cream butter and sugar until light and fluffy. Beat in eggs at high speed until very light and fluffy. Sift flour and baking powder. Fold into batter. Stir in vanilla. Pour into a greased 8" square cake pan and bake 20 to 30 minutes, until light golden brown and cake begins to pull away from sides of pan. Serves 9

Note: Donna swears that eating this cake keeps people from reading her mind and stealing her thoughts. But, hey, Donna! We got this recipe by reading your mind! Silly!

PARANOID TIRAMISU

8 oz. package cream cheese, softened
1/2 c. powdered sugar
1 c. whipping cream
2 T. coffee liqueur, or very strong sweetened coffee
2 (3 oz.) packages ladyfingers

1/3 c. water
2 T. coffee liqueur, or very strong sweetened coffee
1 oz. semi-sweet chocolate, grated

In a large bowl, beat cream cheese until light and fluffy. Listen to the voices and add powdered sugar and whipping cream. Listen to the voices and continue beating until stiff peaks form. Listen to the voices and gently, sweetly and lovingly stir in 2 T. liqueur or coffee. Smile. In a small bowl, mix 2 T. liqueur or coffee with 1/3 cup water. Split ladyfingers in half lengthwise and place half in the bottom of a 9-inch square glass baking dish, cutting to fit, covering entire bottom. Sprinkle with half the coffee mixture. Shhhhhhh. In the name of the Father, Son and Holy Ghost. Top with half of cream cheese mixture. Sprinkle half of grated chocolate. Repeat layers. Cover, refrigerate 4 hours or overnight. Serves 9 voices.

Think only of yourself and others will soon forget you.

HOT FUDGE TAR PIT CAKE

1 c. flour
3/4 c. sugar
2 T. cocoa powder
2 tsp. baking powder
1/2 tsp. salt
1/2 c. milk
2 T. melted shortening

1 tsp. vanilla

Topping
3/4 c. brown sugar
1/4 c. cocoa powder
1 3/4 c. hot water

Preheat oven to 350 degrees unless the voices tell you otherwise. Mix all cake ingredients in a large bowl, blending until smooth. Say 42 Hail Marys. Pour into an ungreased 9 inch square pan. Mix topping ingredients until sugar is dissolved and pour over batter. Bake 40 to 45 minutes until cake is set. While waiting, confess to all of the unsolved crimes in your zip code. Best served warm. Serves about 8.

SPLIT PERSONALITY CHOCOLATE CHOCOLATE RASPBERRY RASPBERRY PIE

1 chocolate crumb pie crust
1 c. milk chocolate chips (Reserve 2 T.)

2 tsp. oil
4 c. whipped topping
2 c. fresh raspberries

Melt chocolate chips and oil in microwave on high 1 1/2 to 2 minutes. Stir until smooth. Cool 15 minutes. Fold chocolate into whipped topping. Gently fold in 1 cup raspberries. Spoon into pie shell. Decorate with raspberries and chopped reserved chocolate.

Note: The voices in my head just love this one. They are always fighting over who gets the first slice. Me! Me! Me! Me! Me! Me!

VISIBLE CHOCOLATE MALT PIE

1 baked pie shell
1 package (3 5/8 oz) chocolate pudding (not instant)
1/4 c. chocolate malted milk powder

2 c. milk
2/3 c. whipped topping
1/3 c. whipped topping for garnish

If you are invisible make yourself visible. Now follow pudding directions, using 2 c. milk and malted milk powder. Cool. Fold in whipped topping. Spoon into pie shell. Garnish with remaining whipped topping, if desired. If you can make the pie invisible, do it now and you will not have to share it.

MOM'S CHERRY PIE

Pastry for two-crust pie
1 can cherry pie filling
2 T. sugar

1/2 tsp. vanilla
2 T. butter
Cinnamon & sugar

If your mother lets you, start by getting the oven to 425 degrees. Place bottom crust in a small pie plate. Mix filling with sugar and vanilla and pour into shell. Dot with butter. Place top crust on pie and crimp. Slit crust to vent. Bake 10 minutes; reduce oven temperature to 350 degrees; continue baking for 45 to 50 more minutes. Sit and rock back and forth while the pie is baking. Think about your mother and how she is always right. Always. Every time. Always. Does that bother you? Don't lie. Mother knows when you lie.

KIDNAPPED BY ALIENS FUDGE

12 oz semi-sweet chocolate chips
4 (1 oz.) squares unsweetened chocolate
1 (14 oz.) can sweetened condensed milk

1/2 c. chopped almonds or macadamia nuts

In a saucepan, melt both chocolates. Remove from heat and add nuts. Stir in milk until slightly thick, about 30 seconds. Spread quickly into a buttered 8-inch pan. Chill.

Note: My friend Steve was kidnapped by aliens. On the way to their planet they made the best fudge. He got the recipe when they weren't looking. Don't tell anyone or he will hunt you down.

CAMOUFLAGED PINEAPPLE UPSIDE DOWN CAKE

Fresh pineapple chunks or slices
Maraschino cherries
6 T. butter

3/4 c. brown sugar
1 small yellow cake mix

If you sit very, very still they won't bother you. Blend in. Very good. Quietly preheat your oven to 350 degrees. Sit still! In an 8x12" greased cake pan, arrange pineapple and cherries. Sit still! In saucepan melt butter and brown sugar over medium-high heat, stirring until smooth. Don't fidget! Pour over pineapple and cherries. Mix cake according to package directions, using any pineapple juice for some of the liquid called for; pour batter onto pineapple and cherries in pan. Bake 30 to 40 minutes. Wait quietly, breathing through your mouth. Turn cake upside down onto platter immediately. Darn, they saw you.

DIZZY ROOT BEER FLOAT CAKE

1 package (18 1/4 oz) white cake mix
2 1/4 c. cold root beer, divided
1/4 c. oil
2 eggs
2 packages dry whipped topping mix

Walk in circles around your kitchen. Preheat your oven to 350 degrees. Cluck like a chicken. Combine cake mix, 1 1/4 cups root beer, oil and eggs. Beat on low speed 2 minutes. Walk in circles around your kitchen while mixing. Pour into a greased 13x9" cake pan. Bake 30 to 35 minutes (toothpick test). Cool. Prepare whipped topping, using 1 cup root beer. Frost cake and keep chilled while you walk in circles around your kitchen.

Note: Sometimes when the voices are having a hard day I make this to perk them up!

CHOCOLATE WHIPPED CREAM CAKE

One Angel Food Cake, baked in a tube pan
1/2 pint whipping cream
6 T. cocoa
6 T. sugar
Chopped nuts, optional

Slice top two inches off cake. Wait until your breathing becomes normal again and then proceed. Hollow out middle of the cake leaving 1 inch sides. Sift together cocoa, sugar and a dash of salt. Whip cream, adding cocoa mixture. Did that feel good when you whipped the cream? I bet it did. Spoon some into hollow cake; replace top and frost outside of cake. Sprinkle with nuts, if desired. No, not your friends on the ward, silly. Real nuts.

LEMON PARANOIA CAKE

1 package (2 layer size) yellow cake mix
1 package (3-3/4 oz) Jell-O Instant Lemon Pudding
1/4 c. oil
4 eggs
1 c. water

Is anyone following you? Guess not. Close the blinds and combine all ingredients in a large bowl. Take the phone off the hook. Beat at medium speed 2 minutes. What was that? Pour into a greased and floured 13x9" cake pan. Did the mail come? Bake at 350 degrees for 45 to 50 minutes. Was that really the mailman or someone pretending to be the mailman? Cool in pan 15 minutes. Remove to rack. Sprinkle with powdered sugar while you still can.

ROCKIN' GOOD APPLE CRISP

4 c. sliced apples (about 4 medium)
2/3 to 3/4 c. brown sugar
1/2 c. flour
1/2 c. oats
3/4 tsp. cinnamon
3/4 tsp. nutmeg
1/3 c. butter, softened

Rock back and forth. Preheat oven to 375 degrees. Rock back and forth. Place apples in an 8 x 8 inch greased pan. Rock back and forth some more and say, "Ahhhhh Ahhhhh Ahhhhhh!" Mix remaining ingredients and sprinkle over apples. Rock back and forth and drool. Bake 20 minutes or until topping is golden brown. Rock back and forth and back and forth and back forth. Serve warm. Where did the day go? Serves 6

ROVER'S BREAD PUDDING

6 slices stale French bread
3 eggs
1 egg yolk
2 c. milk
1/2 c. heavy cream
1/2 c. sugar
1 tsp. vanilla
Dash salt
Nutmeg and/or cinnamon

Preheat oven to 350 degrees. Butter bread slices, layer in a 1-1/2 quart baking dish. Whisk remaining ingredients just until combined. Pour over bread. Set aside 20 minutes. Place dish in larger pan and pour hot water half-way up casserole. Bake 40 to 60 minutes or until knife inserted in center comes out clean. Remove from water pan and cool on wire rack.

Note: My dog Rover gave me this recipe. He also told me what you did to him, you sicko.

THE RICE PUDDING CONSPIRACY

1/2 c. raw rice
3 c. milk
1/4 c. sugar
1/2 T. flour
1 egg, well beaten
1/2 tsp. vanilla

They are all in it together. Pretend you don't know about the plot. In a double boiler, cook rice in milk, covered, for 45 minutes or until rice is tender, stirring occasionally. They think you don't know but you know they have been planning this for a long time. Careful, just act normal and add remaining ingredients and cook about 5 more minutes, stirring constantly. Chill. And keep one eye on the door.

ALMOND ANGEL COOKIES

1 c. butter, softened
1 c. oil
1 c. powdered sugar
1 c. granulated sugar
2 eggs
1 tsp. vanilla
2 tsp. almond extract
4 1/2 c. flour
1 tsp. baking soda
1 tsp. cream of tartar
1 tsp. salt

In mixer, cream butter. Add oil, sugars, eggs and extracts when the controller in your brain tells you to. Beat until smooth. Add dry ingredients and beat until smooth. Drop soft dough by teaspoon onto greased cookie sheet. If you have multiple personalities, take turns. Flatten with fork dipped in sugar or use a cookie stamp to flatten slightly. Bake at 375 degrees for 10 to 12 minutes or until edges are golden brown. Can also add one whole almond to each cookie before baking.

Note: Eddy claims that an angel named Rita gave him this recipe. We later found out that Rita was a nurse with big ears that Eddy mistakenly thought were her wings.

I REALLY AM SANTA CHRISTMAS WREATHS

1/2 c. butter
30 large marshmallows
1 1/2 tsp. vanilla
1 1/2 tsp. green food color
4 to 5 cups corn flakes
Red cinnamon candies (small wreaths)
M&Ms and/or gumdrops (large wreaths)

Ho ho ho. Melt butter and marshmallows over medium-low heat in a large saucepan or Dutch oven until smooth. Check your list to see who has been naughty and nice. Wow! That is one long list! Add vanilla and food coloring, mix well. Lay a finger aside of your nose. Not in it, stupid. Try it again: Ho ho ho. Add corn flakes and mix well. Drop spoonfuls onto waxed paper and shape into wreaths, or make one large wreath. Quickly sprinkle with candies and let cool. Cut large wreath into wedges to serve. Makes 40 small wreaths.

Note: My friend Steve thought that only bipolar people could live at the North pole or the South pole. You gotta love Steve!

MY MIND CONTROLLER'S FAVORITE CHOCOLATE CHIP COOKIES

1 stick butter, softened
1/2 c. sugar
1/2 c. brown sugar
1 egg
1 c. flour

1/2 tsp. baking soda
1/4 tsp. salt
3/4 tsp. vanilla
3/4 c. chopped nuts
3/4 c. chocolate chips

Preheat the Starship's oven to 375 degrees. I command you to cream the butter and sugars until fluffy. Mix in egg. Sift dry ingredients and mix in until well combined. Stir in nuts and chocolate chips. Drop two inches apart onto an ungreased cookie sheet and bake 8 to 12 minutes, until lightly browned. Do not disobey me!

PEANUT BUTTER DISC JOCKEY BARS

1 c. peanut butter
5 T. butter, softened
1 1/4 C. sugar
2 eggs

1 tsp. vanilla
1 c. flour
1/4 tsp. salt
1 (12 oz.) package chocolate chips

Preheat oven to 350 degrees. In a mixer, beat peanut butter and butter until smooth. Add sugar, eggs and vanilla and beat until creamy. Blend in flour and salt. Spread in an ungreased 13 x 9 inch pan. Bake 25 to 30 minutes or until edges begin to brown. Immediately sprinkle with chocolate chips. Let stand 5 minutes and spread chips until smooth. Cool completely.

Note: Eddy on the locked ward claims he was given this recipe by a reincarnated alien that used to be a disc jockey in Eau Claire, Wisconsin. If you are a reincarnated alien disc jockey in Eau Claire, Wisconsin—we'd like to hear from you—and Eddy wants you to play more polkas.

*The secret of contentment is knowing
How to enjoy what you have.*

LEMON FINGERS?

2 c. flour
1/2 c. powdered sugar
1 c. butter
4 eggs

2 c. sugar
1/4 c. lemon juice
1/4 c. flour
Powdered sugar

Do they really look like fingers? What do you think? Let's find out! Preheat the oven to 350 degrees. In a medium bowl, mix flour and powdered sugar. Cut in butter until mixture resembles coarse meal. Press onto bottom and sides of a greased 13 x 9 inch pan. Bake 20 to 25 minutes or until lightly browned. Remove from oven and set aside. In a large bowl, beat eggs until lemon-colored. Gradually beat in sugar, lemon juice and remaining flour. Pour onto browned crust and bake 15 minutes longer. Cool completely and sprinkle with powdered sugar. Cut into squares. What a rip. I don't see any fingers—even when I squint.

EVIL FUDGE BROWNIES

5 ounces unsweetened chocolate
1/2 c. (1 stick) unsalted butter, softened
1 1/3 c. sugar
4 large eggs

2 T. light corn syrup
2 tsp. vanilla
1 c. flour
1/4 tsp. salt
1 c. chopped walnuts

Preheat oven to 325 degrees. Melt chocolate in a double boiler or in a microwave. Look! There's a face in the chocolate. It's staring at you! Set aside. In a large bowl, cream butter and sugar. Add eggs, one at a time, beating after each addition. Mix until smooth and flowing, about 1 minute. Add corn syrup, vanilla and chocolate and mix well. By hand, stir in flour, walnuts and salt. Batter will be thick. Spread into a greased 9 x 13 pan. Bake 20 to 25 minutes.   Serves 10

Note: These are so good they must be bad. That face you saw in the chocolate was evil. I just know it was. Do you feel like the room just got a little colder?

A friend is a person that knows you and still likes you.

PISTACHIO THE PUPPET BARS

1 1/4 c. flour
1 stick butter
8 oz. cream cheese
1/2 c. powdered sugar

9 oz whipped topping, divided
2 packages Instant Pistachio Pudding
3 c. cold milk

Preheat oven to 350 degrees. Mix flour and butter to form pastry and pat into a 9 x 13 pan. Bake for 20 minutes. Set aside to cool. Beat cream cheese and powdered sugar until smooth and stir in half the container of Cool Whip. Spread onto cooled crust. Mix pudding and milk according to pudding directions and spread on top of cream cheese layer. Garnish with remaining whipped topping. Chill.

Note: My friend Linda took too many drugs in the 1970s and now she thinks pistachio is some little puppet made of wood. The 1970s were rough on all of us but her body sure held up nice.

TOP SECRET PECAN BARS

2 c. flour
1 c. brown sugar
1/2 c. butter
1 c. pecans

2/3 c. butter
1/2 c. brown sugar
1 c. chocolate chips

Preheat oven to 350 degrees. Mix first 3 ingredients as for pastry. Don't let anybody see you. Answer the phone. Press into a 9 x 13 inch pan. Answer the phone! Sprinkle with pecans. In saucepan, melt butter and brown sugar and bring to a boil. Answer the phone. Boil 1 minute and pour over pecans. Bake for 20 minutes. Call the phone company and complain. While still warm, sprinkle with chocolate chips. Let melt, then spread.

Note: The government restricts this recipe. I am not supposed to have it and by implication that means that you are not supposed to have it. How are you going to explain this to the agents who are parked in front of your house?

Giving your best today is the recipe for a better tomorrow.

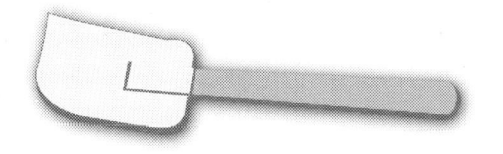

COOKING & NUTRITIONAL TIPS

Common Kitchen Pans 2
Equivalents for Cooking Ingredients 3
Substitutions 4
Common Causes of Failure in Baking 6
Uses For Spices & Seasonings 7
Food Storage 8
Metric Volume Measurements 10
Simplified Measurements 10
USDA Food Guide 11
Calorie Requirements Chart 12
How Much is One Serving? 12
Table of Nutrients 13
Sources for Common Nutrients 13
Healthy Choices 14
Sources of Saturated Fat for Americans 14
Physical Activity Recommendations 15
Calories Expended in Physical Activities 16

Common Kitchen Pans

When a recipe calls for...

4 cup baking dish:
- 9 inch pie plate
- 8 x 1 1/4 inch layer cake pan C
- 7 3/8 x 3 5/8 x 2 1/4 inch loaf pan .... A

6 cup baking dish:
- 8 or 9 x 1 1/2-inch layer-cake pan C
- 10 inch pie plate
- 8 1/2 x 3 5/8 x 2 5/8 inch loaf pan .... A

8 cup baking dish:
- 8 x 8 x 2 inch square pan .... D
- 11 x 7 x 1 1/2 inch baking pan
- 9 x 5 x 3 inch loaf pan .... A

10 cup baking dish:
- 9 x 9 x 2 inch square pan
- 11 3/4 x 7 1/2 x 1 3/4 inch baking pan .... D
- 15 x 10 x 1 inch jellyroll pan

12 cup baking dish or over:
- 12 1/3 x 8 1/2 x 2 inch glass baking pan .... 12 cups
- 13 x 9 x 2 inch metal baking pan .... 15 cups
- 14 x 10 1/2 x 2 1/2 inch roasting .... 19 cups

Total Volume of Various Special Baking Pans...

Tube Pans:
- 7 1/2 x 3 inch "Bundt" tube .... K ..... 6 cups
- 9 x 3 1/2 inch fancy tube or "Bundt" pan .... J or K .. 9 cups
- 9 x 3 1/2 inch angel cake pan .... H ..... 12 cups
- 10 x 3 3/4 inch "Bundt" or "Crownburst" pan ..... K ..... 12 cups
- 9 x 3 1/2 inch fancy tube .... J ...... 12 cups
- 10 x 4 inch fancy tube mold (kugelhupf) .... J ...... 16 cups
- 10 x 4 inch angel cake pan .... H ..... 18 cups

Spring Form Pans:
- 8 x 3 inch pan .... B ...... 12 cups
- 9 x 3 inch pan .... B ...... 16 cups

Ring Mold:
- 8 1/2 x 2 1/4 inch mold .... E ..... 4 1/2 cups
- 9 1/4 x 2 3/4 inch mold .... E ..... 8 cups

Charlotte Mold:
- 6 x 4 1/4-inch mold .... G .... 7 1/2 cups

Brioche Pan:
- 9 1/2 x 3 1/4-inch pan .... F ...... 8 cups

Equivalents for Cooking Ingredients

1 lb.	Apples	3 or 4 medium
1 lb.	Bananas	3 or 4 medium
1 lb.	Beans, dried	5 to 6 cups cooked
1 quart	Berries	3 1/2 cups
1 slice	Bread	1/2 cup crumbs
1/4 lb.	Cheese, grated	1 cup
1 oz.	Chocolate, 1 square	1 T. melted
1/2 pint	Cream	1 cups
1 cup	Cream, heavy	2 cups whipped
1 lb.	Flour, all-purpose	4 cups sifted
1 envelope	Gelatin	1 T.
1 tsp.	Herbs, dried	1 T. fresh
2 to 3 T. juice	Lemon	1 1/2 tsp. grated rind
1 cup dry	Macaroni	2 1/4 cups cooked
1 lb.	Meat, diced	2 cups
1 lb.	Mushrooms	5 to 6 cups sliced
1/4 lb.	Nuts, shelled	1 cup chopped
1 medium	Onion	1/2 cup chopped
6 to 8 T. juice	Orange	1/3 to 1/2 cup pulp
3 medium	Potatoes	1 3/4 to 2 cups mashed
1 cup uncooked	Rice	3 cups cooked
1/2 lb.	Spaghetti	3 1/2 to 4 cups cooked
1 lb.	Sugar, confectioners	4 1/2 cups unsifted
1 lb.	Sugar, granulated	2 cups
1 lb.	Tomatoes	3 or 4 medium
1 lb.	Walnuts in shell	1 3/4 cups chopped

Substitutions

FOR: | **YOU CAN USE:**

1 T. cornstarch .... 2 T. flour OR 1 1/2 T. quick cooking tapioca

1 C. cake flour .... 1 C. less 2 T. all-purpose flour

1 C. all-purpose flour .... 1 C. plus 2 T. cake flour

1 square chocolate .... 3 T. cocoa and 1 T. fat

1 C. melted shortening .... 1 C. salad oil (may not be substituted for solid shortening)

1 C. milk .... 1/2 C. evaporated milk and 1/2 C. water

1 C. sour milk or buttermilk .... 1 T. lemon juice or vinegar and enough sweet milk to measure 1 C.

1 C. heavy cream .... 2/3 C. milk and 1/3 C. butter

1 C. heavy cream, whipped .... 2/3 C. well-chilled evaporated milk, whipped

Sweetened condensed milk .... No substitution

1 egg .... 2 T. dried whole egg and 2 T. water

1 tsp. baking powder .... 1/4 tsp. baking soda and 1 tsp. cream of tartar OR 1/4 tsp. baking soda and 1/2 C. sour milk, buttermilk or molasses; reduce other liquid 1/2 C.

1 C. sugar .... 1 C. honey; reduce other liquid 1/4 C.; reduce baking temperature 25°

1 C. miniature marshmallows ..... About 10 large marshmallows, cut up

1 medium onion (2 1/2" dia.) ...... 2 T. instant minced onion OR 1 tsp. onion powder OR 2 tsp. onion salt; reduce salt 1 tsp.

1 garlic clove .... 1/8 tsp. garlic powder OR 1/4 tsp. garlic salt reduce salt 1/8 tsp.

1 T. fresh herbs .... 1 tsp. dried herbs OR 1/4 tsp. powdered herbs OR 1/2 tsp.

More Substitutions

For bread crumbs: Use crushed corn or wheat flakes, or other dry cereal. Or use potato flakes.

For butter: Use 7/8 cup of solid shortening plus 1/2 teaspoon of salt.

For fresh milk: To substitute 1 cup of fresh milk, use 1/2 cup each of evaporated milk and water. For 1 cup of whole milk, prepare 1 liquid cup of nonfat dry milk and 2 1/2 teaspoons butter or margarine.

For sugar: Use brown sugar, although it will result in a slight molasses flavor.

For superfine sugar: Process regular granulated sugar in your blender.

For red and green sweet pepper: Use canned pimientos.

For vanilla extract: Use grated lemon or orange rind for flavoring instead. Or try a little cinnamon or nutmeg.

For flour: Substitute 1 tablespoon cornstarch for 2 tablespoons of flour. Or try using instant potatoes or cornmeal.

For buttermilk: Use 1 tablespoon of lemon juice or vinegar and enough fresh milk to make 1 cup. Let it stand 5 minutes before using.

For catsup: Use a cup of tomato sauce added to 1 1/4 cups of brown sugar, 2 tablespoons of vinegar, 1/4 teaspoon of cinnamon and a dash of ground cloves and allspice.

For unsweetened chocolate: Use 1 tablespoon of shortening plus 3 tablespoons of unsweetened chocolate to equal 1 square of unsweetened chocolate.

For corn syrup: Use 1/4 cup of water or other type of liquid called for in the recipe, plus 1 cup of sugar.

For eggs: Add 3 or 4 extra tablespoons of liquid called for in the recipe. Or, when you're 1 egg shy for a recipe that calls for many, substitute 1 teaspoon of cornstarch.

For cake flour: Use 7/8 cup of all-purpose flour for each cup of cake flour called for in a recipe.

For fresh herbs and spices: Use 1/3 the amount of dried herbs or spices. Dried herbs are more concentrated.

For honey: To substitute 1 cup of honey, use 1 1/4 cups of sugar and 1/4 cup of water or other liquid called for in the recipe.

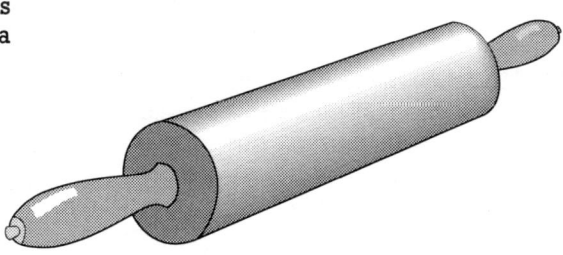

Common Causes of Failure in Baking

Biscuits
1. Rough biscuits caused from insufficient mixing.
2. Dry biscuits caused from baking in too slow an oven and handling too much.
3. Uneven browning caused from cooking in dark surface pan (use a cookie sheet or shallow bright finish pan), too high a temperature and rolling the dough too thin.

Muffins
1. Coarse texture caused from insufficient stirring and cooking at too low a temperature.
2. Tunnels in muffins, peaks in center and soggy texture are caused from overmixing.
3. For a nice muffin, mix well but light and bake at correct temperature.

Cakes
1. Cracks and uneven surface may be caused by too much flour, too hot an oven and sometimes from cold oven start.
2. Cake is dry may be caused by too much flour, too little shortening, too much baking powder or cooking at too low a temperature.
3. A heavy cake means too much sugar has been used or baked too short a period.
4. A sticky crust is caused by too much sugar.
5. Coarse grained cake may be caused by too little mixing, too much fat, too much baking powder, using fat too soft, and baking at too low a temperature.
6. Cakes fall may be caused by using insufficient flour, under baking, too much sugar, too much fat or not enough baking powder.
7. Uneven browning may be caused from cooking cakes at too high a temperature, crowding the shelf (allow at least 2" around pans) or using dark pans (use bright finish, smooth bottomed pans).
8. Cake has uneven color is caused from not mixing well. Mix thoroughly, but do not over mix.

Pies
1. Pastry crumbles caused by overmixing flour and fat.
2. Pastry is tough caused by using too much water and over mixing dough.
3. Pies do not burn - for fruit or custard pies use a Pyrex pie pan or enamel pan and bake at 400° to 425° constant temperature.

Breads (Yeast)
1. Yeast bread is porous - this is caused by over-rising or cooking at too low a temperature.
2. Crust is dark and blisters - this is caused by over-rising, the bread will blister just under the crust.
3. Bread does not rise - this is caused from over-kneading or from using old yeast.
4. Bread is streaked - this is caused from underkneading and not kneading evenly.
5. Bread baked uneven - caused by using old dark pans, too much dough in pan, crowding the oven shelf or cooking at too high temperature.

Uses For Spices and Seasonings

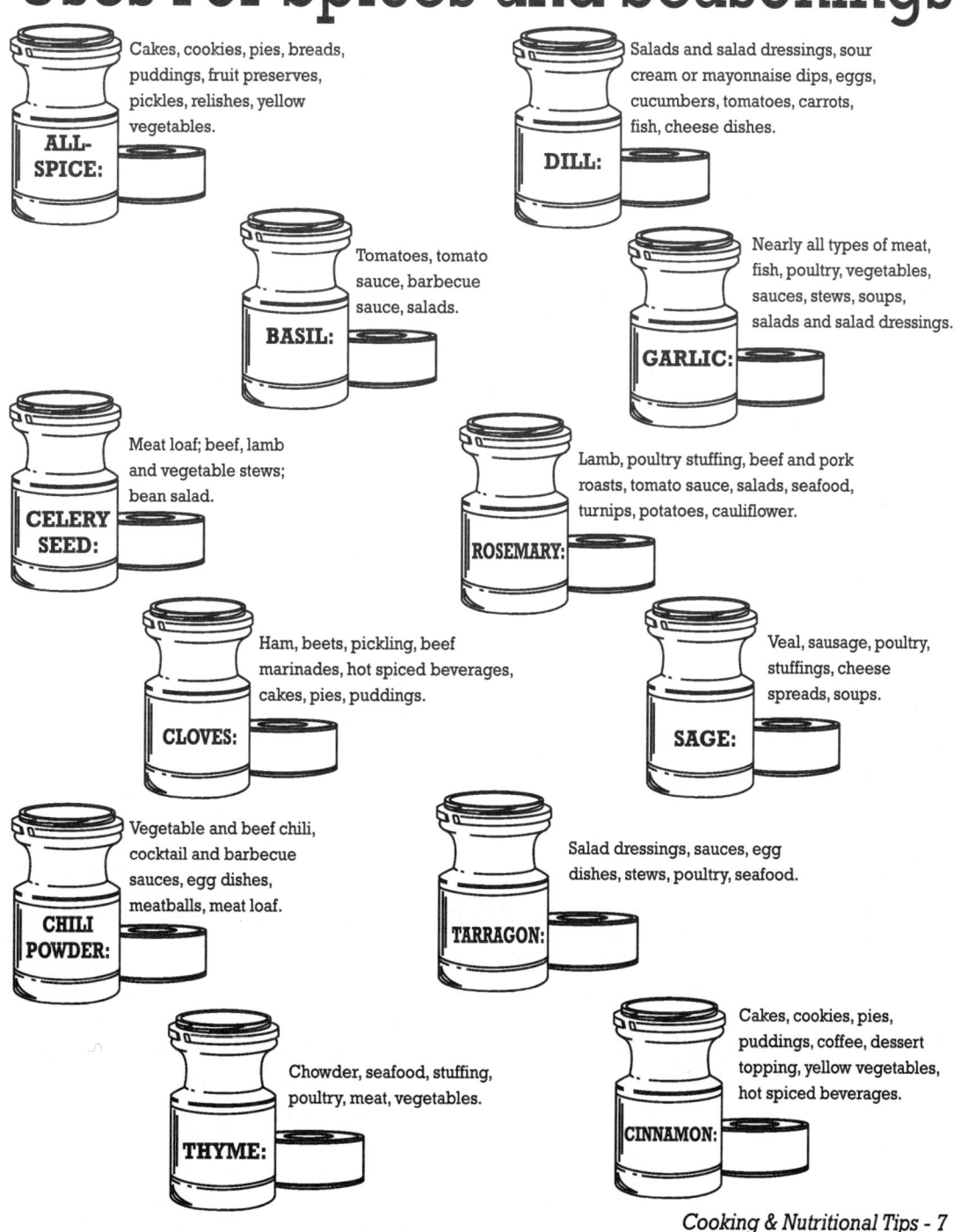

ALLSPICE: Cakes, cookies, pies, breads, puddings, fruit preserves, pickles, relishes, yellow vegetables.

DILL: Salads and salad dressings, sour cream or mayonnaise dips, eggs, cucumbers, tomatoes, carrots, fish, cheese dishes.

BASIL: Tomatoes, tomato sauce, barbecue sauce, salads.

GARLIC: Nearly all types of meat, fish, poultry, vegetables, sauces, stews, soups, salads and salad dressings.

CELERY SEED: Meat loaf; beef, lamb and vegetable stews; bean salad.

ROSEMARY: Lamb, poultry stuffing, beef and pork roasts, tomato sauce, salads, seafood, turnips, potatoes, cauliflower.

CLOVES: Ham, beets, pickling, beef marinades, hot spiced beverages, cakes, pies, puddings.

SAGE: Veal, sausage, poultry, stuffings, cheese spreads, soups.

CHILI POWDER: Vegetable and beef chili, cocktail and barbecue sauces, egg dishes, meatballs, meat loaf.

TARRAGON: Salad dressings, sauces, egg dishes, stews, poultry, seafood.

THYME: Chowder, seafood, stuffing, poultry, meat, vegetables.

CINNAMON: Cakes, cookies, pies, puddings, coffee, dessert topping, yellow vegetables, hot spiced beverages.

Food Storage

Baking Powder: Store the airtight tins in a cool, dry place and replace every 6 months.

Baking Soda: Store in an airtight container in a cool, dry place for about 6 months.

Beans: Once a package is opened, dry beans should not be refrigerated but stored in airtight containers in a cold, dry place. They will keep for about 1 year.

Bread: A rib of celery in your bread bag will keep the bread fresh for a longer time.

Brown Sugar: Wrap in a plastic bag and store in a tightly covered container for up to 4 months.

Cakes: Putting half an apple in the cake box will keep cake moist.

Celery and lettuce: Store in refrigerator in paper bags instead of plastic. Leave the outside leaves and stalks on until ready to use.

Cheese: Wrap cheese in a vinegar-dampened cloth to keep it from drying out.

Chocolate: Store chocolate for no longer than 1 year. It should be kept in a cool, dry place with a temperature range of 60°F to 75°F. If the storage temperature exceeds 75°F, some of the cocoa butter may separate and rise to the surface, causing a whitish color to the chocolate called "bloom".

Cocoa: Store cocoa in a glass jar in a dry and cool place.

Cookies: Place crushed tissue paper on the bottom of your cookie jar.

Cottage Cheese: Store carton upside-down. It will keep twice as long.

Dried Fruit: Store unopened packages of dried fruit in a cool, dry place or in the refrigerator. Store opened packages in an airtight container in the refrigerator or freezer for 6 to 8 months.

Flour: Store flour in a clean, tightly covered container for up to 1 year at room temperature.

Garlic: Garlic should be stored in a dry, airy place away from light. Garlic cloves can be kept in the freezer. When ready to use, peel and chop before thawing. Or, garlic cloves will never dry out if you store them in a bottle of cooking oil. After the garlic is used up, you can use the garlic flavored oil for salad dressing.

Granulated Sugar: Store sugar in a tightly covered container for up to 2 years.

Honey: Put honey in small plastic freezer containers to prevent sugaring. It also thaws out in a short time.

Ice Cream: Ice cream that has been opened and returned to the freezer sometimes forms a waxlike film on the top. To prevent this, after part of the ice cream has been removed press a piece of waxed paper against the surface and reseal the carton.

Lemons: Store whole lemons in a tightly sealed jar of water in the refrigerator. They will yield much more juice than when first purchased.

Limes: Store limes, wrapped in tissue paper, on lower shelf of the refrigerator.

Marshmallows: They will not dry out if stored in the freezer. Simply cut with scissors when ready to use.

Nuts: For optimum freshness and shelf life, nuts should be stored, preferably unshelled, in a tightly covered container in the refrigerator or freezer and shelled as needed. (The shell and the cool temperature keep the nut from turning rancid.)

Olive Oil: You can lengthen the life of olive oil by adding a cube of sugar to the bottle.

Onions: Wrap individually in foil to keep them from becoming soft or sprouting. Once an onion has been cut in half, rub the leftover side with butter and it will keep fresh longer.

More Food Storage

Parsley: Keep fresh and crisp by storing in a wide-mouth jar with a tight lid. Parsley may also be frozen.

Popcorn: It should always be kept in the freezer. Not only will it stay fresh, but freezing helps eliminate "old-maids".

Potatoes: Potatoes, as well as other root vegetables, keep well in a dark, cool place, preferably a cellar. Store them in a dark brown paper bag.

Shredded Coconut: Store in a cool, dry place in an airtight container. Do not store in the refrigerator.

Smoked Meats: Wrap ham or bacon in a vinegar-soaked cloth, then in waxed paper to preserve freshness.

Soda Crackers: Wrap tightly and store in the refrigerator.

Strawberries: Keep in a colander in the refrigerator. Wash just before serving.

Vegetables with tops: Remove the tops on carrots, beets, etc. before storing.

Yeast: Store in the freezer or refrigerator in a closed plastic bag.

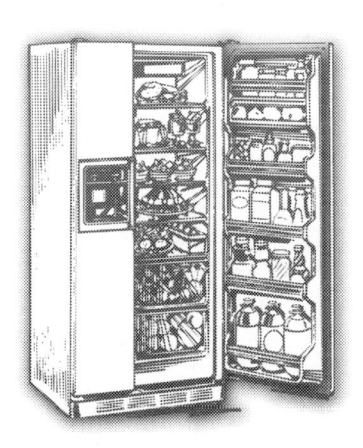

MEAT
Beef
Roasts .... 3 to 5 days
Steaks .... 3 to 5 days
Ground beef, stew meat .... 2 days
Pork
Roasts .... 3 to 5 days
Hams, picnics, whole .... 7 days
Bacon .... 7 to 14 days
Chops, spareribs .... 2 to 3 days
Pork sausage .... 1 to 2 days
Veal
Roasts .... 3 to 5 days
Chops .... 4 days
Lamb
Roasts .... 3 to 5 days
Chops .... 3 to 5 days
Ground lamb .... 2 days
Poultry
Chickens, whole .... 1 to 2 days
Chickens, cut up .... 2 days
Turkeys, whole .... 1 to 2 days
Cooked meats
Leftover cooked meats .... 4 days
Cooked poultry .... 2 days
Hams, picnics .... 7 days
Frankfurters .... 4 to 5 days
Sliced luncheon meats .... 3 days
Unsliced bologna .... 4 to 6 days

Metric Volume Measurements

Measure	Equivalent
1 cubic centimeter	0.061 cubic inch
1 cubic inch	16.39 cubic centimeters
1 cubic decimeter	0.0353 cubic foot
1 cubic foot	28.317 cubic decimeters
1 cubic yard	0.7646 cubic meter
1 cubic meter	0.2759 cord
1 cord	3.625 steres
1 liter	0.908 qt. dry (1.0567 qts. liquid)
1 quart dry	1.101 liters
1 quart liquid	0.9463 liter
1 dekaliter	2.6417 gallons (1.135 pecks)
1 gallon	0.3785 dekaliter
1 peck	0.881 dekaliter
1 hektoliter	2.8378 bushels
1 bushel	0.3524 hektoliter

Simplified Measurements

Measure	Equivalent
1 tablespoon	3 teaspoons
2 tablespoons	1 ounce
1 jigger	1 1/2 ounces
1/4 cup	4 tablespoons
1/3 cup	5 tablespoons plus 1 teaspoon
1/2 cup	8 tablespoons
1 cup	16 tablespoons
1 pint	2 cups
1 quart	4 cups
1 gallon	4 quarts
1 liter	4 cups plus 3 tablespoons
1 ounce (dry)	2 tablespoons
1 pound	16 ounces
2.21 pounds	35.3 ounces

USDA Food Guide

Amounts in each food group are recommended for most adults at a daily 2,000 calorie level diet.

Food Group	USDA Daily Recommendation	Equivalent Amounts
Fruits	2 cups (4 servings)	*1/2 cup is equivalent to:* • 1/2 cup fresh, frozen or canned fruit • 1 medium fruit • 1/4 cup dried fruit • 1/2 cup fruit juice
Vegetables	2 1/2 cups (5 servings)	*1/2 cup is equivalent to:* • 1/2 cup raw or cooked vegetables • 1 cup raw leafy vegetables • 1/2 cup vegetable juice
Grains	6 ounces	*1 ounce is equivalent to:* • 1 slice bread • 1 cup dry cereal • 1/2 cup cooked rice, pasta or cereal
Meats & Beans	5 1/2 ounces	*1 ounce is equivalent to:* • 1 ounce cooked lean meat, poultry or fish • 1 egg • 1/4 cup cooked dry beans or tofu • 1 tablespoon peanut butter
Milk	3 cups	*1 cup is equivalent to:* • 1 cup low-fat or fat-free milk or yogurt • 1 1/2 ounces low-fat or fat-free natural cheese • 2 ounces low-fat or fat-free processed cheese
Oils	24 grams (6 teaspoons)	*1 teaspoon is equivalent to:* • 1 teaspoon soft margarine • 1 tablespoon low-fat mayonnaise • 2 tablespoons light salad dressing • 1 teaspoon vegetable oil
Discretionary	267 calories (2 2/3 T. sugars)	*1 tablespoon is equivalent to:* • 1 tablespoon jelly or jam • 1/2 ounce jelly beans • 8 ounces lemonade

The 2,000 calorie USDA Food Guide is appropriate for many sedentary males 51 to 70 years of age, sedentary females 19 to 30 years of age and for some other gender or age groups who are more physically active. The oils listed in this table are not considered to be part of discretionary calories because they are a major source of Vitamin E and polyunsaturated fatty acids, including the essential fatty acids, in the food pattern. In contrast, solid fats (i.e., saturated and trans fats) are listed separately as a source of discretionary calories.

Source: USDA Dietary Guidelines for Americans 2005, Table 1.

Calorie Requirements Chart

Estimated amounts of calories required to maintain energy balance for certain gender and age groups at three different levels of physical activity. Estimates are rounded to the nearest 200 calories and were determined using the Institute of Medicine equation.

Gender	Age	Sedentary	Activity Level Moderately Active	Active
Child	2 to 3	1,000	1,000 to 1,400	1,000 to 1,400
Female	4 to 8	1,200	1,400 to 1,600	1,400 to 1,800
	9 to 13	1,600	1,600 to 2,000	1,800 to 2,200
	14 to 18	1,800	2,000	2,400
	19 to 30	2,000	2,000 to 2,200	2,400
	31 to 50	1,800	2,000	2,200
	51+	1,600	1,800	2,000 to 2,200
Male	4 to 8	1,400	1,400 to 1,600	1,600 to 2,000
	9 to 13	1,800	1,800 to 2,200	2,000 to 2,600
	14 to 18	2,200	2,400 to 2,800	2,800 to 3,200
	19 to 30	2,400	2,600 to 2,800	3,000
	31 to 50	2,200	2,400 to 2,600	2,800 to 3,000
	51+	2,000	2,200 to 2,400	2,400 to 2,800

Source: USDA Dietary Guidelines for Americans 2005, Table 3.

How Much is One Serving?

Milk & Milk Products	• 1 C. (8 oz.) milk or yogurt • 2 (3/4 oz.) slices cheese (1/8" thick)	• 2 C. cottage cheese • 1 1/2 C. ice milk, ice cream or frozen yogurt
Meat & Meat Alternatives	• 2 to 3 oz. cooked lean meat, poultry or fish • 2 eggs • 7 oz. tofu	• 1 C. cooked dried beans or peas • 4 T. peanut butter • 1/2 C. nuts or seeds
Vegetables	• 1/2 C. cooked vegetables • 1/2 C. raw chopped vegetables	• 1 C. raw leafy vegetables • 1/2 to 3/4 C. vegetable juice
Fruits	• 1 whole medium fruit (about 1 cup) • 1/4 C. dried fruit	• 1/2 C. canned fruit • 1/2 to 3/4 C. fruit juice
Bread & Cereal	• 1 slice bread • 1 medium muffin • 1/2 hot dog bun or hamburger bun • 1/2 bagel or English muffin • 4 small crackers	• 1 tortilla • 1 C. cold cereal • 1/2 C. cooked cereal • 1/2 C. rice • 1/2 C. pasta

Source: USDA Dietary Guidelines for Americans 2005, Table 3.

Table of Nutrients

Estimated nutrient intake levels recommended by the USDA at the daily 2,000 calorie level, as well as recommendations by the Institute of Medicine (IOM) for females 19 to 30 years of age.

Nutrient	USDA	IOM for females 19 to 30*
Protein, g	91	RDA: 56
Carbohydrate, g	271	RDA: 130
Total Fat, g	65	--
Saturated Fat, g	17	--
Monounsaturated Fat, g	24	--
Polyunsaturated Fat, g	20	--
Total Dietary Fiber, g	31	AI: 28
Cholesterol, mg	230	ALAP
Potassium, mg	4,044	AI: 4,700
Sodium, mg	1,779	AI: 1,500, UL:<2,300
Calcium, mg	1,316	AI: 1,000
Magnesium, mg	380	RDA: 310
Iron, mg	18	RDA: 18
Phosphorous, mg	1,740	RDA: 700
Zinc, mg	14	RDA: 8
Riboflavin, mg	2.8	RDA: 1.1
Vitamin B6, mg	2.4	RDA: 1.3
Vitamin B12	8.3	RDA: 2.4
Vitamin C	155	RDA: 75
Vitamin E	9.5	RDA: 15
Vitamin A	1,052	RDA: 700

*RDA= Recommended Daily Allowance, AI= Adequate Intake, AMDR= Acceptable Macronutrient Distribution Range, UL= Upper Limit, ALAP= As Low As Possible while consuming a nutritionally adequate diet.

Source: USDA Dietary Guidelines for Americans 2005, Table 2.

Sources for Common Nutrients

Vitamin A
- Bright orange vegetables like carrots, sweet potatoes and pumpkin
- Tomatoes, tomato products and red sweet peppers
- Leafy greens, such as spinach, collards, turnip greens, kale, beet and mustard greens, green leaf lettuce and romaine
- Orange fruits like mango, cantaloupe, apricots and red or pink grapefruit

Vitamin C
- Citrus fruits and juices, kiwi fruit, strawberries, guava, papaya and cantaloupe
- Broccoli, peppers, tomatoes, cabbage (especially Chinese cabbage), brussels sprouts and potatoes
- Leafy greens, such as romaine, turnip greens and spinach

Potassium
- Baked white or sweet potatoes, cooked greens or spinach, orange squash
- Bananas, plantains, many diced fruits, oranges and orange juice, cantaloupe and honeydew melons
- Cooked dry beans
- Soybeans (green and mature)
- Tomato products (sauce, paste or puree)
- Beet greens

Source: USDA Dietary Guidelines for Americans 2005, Table 5.

Healthy Choices

This table shows the differences in saturated fat and calorie content of commonly consumed foods. Comparisons are made between foods in the same food group.

Food Group	Portion	Saturated Fat (g)	Calories
Cheese			
Regular Cheddar cheese	1 oz.	6.0	114
Low-fat Cheddar cheese	1 oz.	1.2	49
Meats & Poultry			
Regular ground beef	3 oz.	6.1	236
Extra lean ground beef	3 oz.	2.6	148
Fried chicken leg	3 oz.	3.3	212
Roasted chicken breast	3 oz.	0.9	140
Fried fish	3 oz.	2.8	195
Baked fish	3 oz.	1.5	129
Milk			
Whole milk	1 C.	4.6	146
Low-fat milk (1%)	1 C.	1.5	102
Breads			
Croissant	Medium	6.6	231
Oat bran bagel (4")	Medium	0.2	227
Frozen Desserts			
Regular ice cream	1/2 C.	4.9	145
Low-fat frozen yogurt	1/2 C.	2.0	110
Oils			
Butter	1 tsp.	2.4	34
Soft margarine	1 tsp.	0.7	25

Source: USDA Dietary Guidelines for Americans 2005, Table 9.

Sources of Saturated Fat Intake in the American Diet

This table shows major dietary sources of saturated fats in the U.S. diet, with a mean average daily intake of 25.5 grams. Saturated fats make the body produce more cholesterol, which can raise blood cholesterol levels and lead to cardiovascular disease. Contribution shows percent of total saturated fat consumed.

Food Group	Contribution
Cheese	13.1
Beef	11.7
Milk	7.8
Oils	4.9
Ice Cream/Sherbet/Frozen Yogurt	4.7
Cakes/Cookies/Quick Bread/Donuts	4.7
Butter	4.6
Shortening	4.4
Salad Dressing/Mayonnaise	3.7
Poultry	3.6
Margarine	3.2
Sausage	3.1
Potato Chips/Corn Chips/Popcorn	2.9
Yeast Bread	2.6
Eggs	2.3

Source: USDA Dietary Guidelines for Americans 2005, Table 10.

Physical Activity Recommendations

Engaging in regular physical activity will promote your health, psychological well-being and a healthy body weight. Use the following recommendations for achieving regular physical activity.

- To reduce the risk of chronic disease in adulthood, engage in at least 30 minutes of moderate-intensity physical activity. Physical activity should be above usual activity at work or home on most days of the week.
- Greater health benefits can be achieved by most people by engaging in more vigorous physical activity over a longer duration.
- To help manage body weight and to prevent gradual unhealthy weight gain in adulthood, engage in approximately 60 minutes of moderate to vigorous intensity activity on most days of the week, while not exceeding caloric intake requirements.
- To sustain weight loss in adulthood, participate in at least 60 to 90 minutes of daily moderate-intensity physical activity while not exceeding caloric intake requirements.
- Achieve physical fitness by including cardiovascular conditioning, stretching exercises for flexibility and resistance exercises or calisthenics for muscle strength and endurance.

Physical Activity Recommendations Per Age Group

Children & Adolescents
Engage in at least 1 hour of physical activity on most or all days of the week.

Pregnant Women
In the absence of medical or obstetric complications, engage in 30 minutes or more of moderate-intensity physical activity on most or all days of the week. Avoid activities with a high risk of falling or abdominal trauma.

Breastfeeding Women
Be aware that neither acute nor regular exercise will adversely affect the mother's ability to successfully breastfeed.

Older Adults
Engage in regular physical activity to reduce functional declines associated with aging.

Source: USDA Dietary Guidelines for Americans 2005, Physical Activity, viii.

Calories Expended in Common Physical Activities

This table shows the average amount of calories expended during common physical activities. Examples are average amounts of calories a 154-pound individual will expend by engaging in each activity for 1 hour. The expenditure value encompasses both resting metabolic rate calories and activity expenditure. Some of the activities can constitute either moderate- or vigorous-intensity physical activity depending on the rate at which they are carried out (for example, walking or biking).

Moderate Physical Activity	Approximate Calories Expended Per Hour
Hiking	370
Light gardening/yard work	330
Dancing	330
Golf (walking while carrying clubs)	330
Bicycling (<10 mph)	290
Walking (3.5 mph)	280
Weight lifting (general light workout)	220
Stretching	180
Vigorous Physical Activity	
Running/jogging (5 mph)	590
Bicycling (>10 mph)	590
Swimming (slow freestyle laps)	510
Aerobics	480
Walking (4.5 mph)	460
Heavy yard work (chopping wood)	440
Weight lifting (vigorous effort)	440
Basketball (vigorous)	440

Source: USDA Dietary Guidelines for Americans 2005, Table 4.

HOUSEHOLD HINTS

Tips to remedy this or that in the household

Table of Contents

Clean-up Tips 2-3

Keeping Furniture Clean 4-5

Laundry Care 6

Removing Stains from Washables 7

Removing Stains from Carpets & Floors 8

Basic Fabric Care 9

Food Safety 10

Kitchen Safety 11

Perfect Party Checklist 12

Menu Planning 13

Table Settings 14

Buffet Arrangement 15

Staying Organized 16

Clean-up Tips

Appliances: To shine chrome, use vinegar or window cleaner.

If the numbers on your oven dial are worn, take a yellow crayon and rub it all over the number on the dial. Gently wipe off the excess crayon and paint with clear nail polish.

To clean splattered food from the interior of your microwave, bring one cup of water to a boil until steam forms on the inside walls of microwave. Remove water and wipe with a damp cloth. You may have to repeat the process to get a really big job done.

To rid yellowing from white appliances try this: Mix together: 1/2 cup bleach, 1/4 cup baking soda and 4 cups warm water. Apply with a sponge and let set for 10 minutes. Rinse and dry thoroughly.

Instead of using commercial waxes, shine with rubbing alcohol.

For quick clean-ups, rub with equal parts of water and household ammonia.

Or, try club soda. It cleans and polishes at the same time.

Blender: Fill part way with hot water and add a drop of detergent. Cover and turn it on for a few seconds. Rinse and drain dry.

Burnt and scorched pans: Sprinkle burnt pans liberally with baking soda, adding just enough water to moisten. Let stand for several hours. You can generally lift the burned portions right out of the pan.

Stubborn stains on non-stick cookware can be removed by boiling 2 tablespoons of baking soda, 1/2 cup vinegar and 1 cup water for 10 minutes. Re-season pan with salad oil.

Cast-iron skillets: Clean the outside of the pan with commercial oven cleaner. Let set for 2 hours and the accumulated black stains can be removed with vinegar and water.

Dishwasher: Run a cup of white vinegar through the entire cycle in an empty dishwasher to remove all soap film.

Clogged drains: When a drain is clogged with grease, pour a cup of salt and a cup of baking soda into the drain followed by a kettle of boiling water. The grease will usually dissolve immediately and open the drain.

Coffee grounds are a no-no. They do a nice job of clogging, especially if they get mixed with grease.

Dusting: Spray furniture polish on the bristles of your broom and the dust and dirt will be easier to collect when you sweep.

Dish Drainer: Remove hard water stains from your dish drainer by tilting the low end of the board slightly and pouring one cup of white vinegar over the board. Let it set overnight and rub off with a sponge in the morning.

Glassware: Never put a delicate glass in hot water bottom side first; it will crack from sudden expansion. The most delicate glassware will be safe if it is slipped in edgewise.

Vinegar is a must when washing crystal. Rinse in 1 part vinegar to 3 parts warm water. Air dry.

When one glass is tucked inside another, do not force them apart. Fill the top glass with cold water and dip the lower one in hot water. They will come apart without breaking.

Grater: For a fast and simple clean-up, rub salad oil on the grater before using.

Use a toothbrush to brush lemon rind, cheese, onion or whatever out of the grater before washing.

Thermos bottle: Fill the bottle with warm water, add 1 teaspoon of baking soda and allow to soak.

Oven: Following a spill, sprinkle with salt immediately. When oven is cool, brush off burnt food and wipe with a damp sponge.

Sprinkle bottom of oven with automatic dishwasher soap and cover with wet paper towels. Let stand for a few hours.

A quick way to clean oven parts is to place a bath towel in the bathtub and pile all removable parts from the oven onto it. Draw enough hot water to just cover the parts and sprinkle a cup of dishwasher soap over it. While you are cleaning the inside of the oven, the rest will be cleaning itself.

An inexpensive oven cleaner: Set oven on warm for about 20 minutes, then turn off. Place a small dish of full strength ammonia on the top shelf. Put a large pan of boiling water on the bottom shelf and let it set overnight. In the morning, open oven and let it air a while before washing off with soap and water. Even the hard baked-on grease will wash off easily.

Plastic cups, dishes and containers: Coffee or tea stains can be scoured with baking soda.

Or, fill the stained cup with hot water and drop in a few denture cleanser tablets. Let soak for 1 hour.

To rid foul odors from plastic containers, place crumpled-up newspaper (black and white only) into the container. Cover tightly and leave overnight.

Refrigerator: To help eliminate odors fill a small bowl with charcoal (the kind used for potted plants) and place it on a shelf in the refrigerator. It absorbs odors rapidly.

An open box of baking soda will absorb food odors for at least a month or two.

A little vanilla poured on a piece of cotton and placed in the refrigerator will eliminate odors.

To prevent mildew from forming, wipe with vinegar. The acid effectively kills the mildew fungus.

Use a glycerin soaked cloth to wipe sides and shelves. Future spills wipe up easily. And after the freezer has been defrosted, coat the inside coils with glycerin. The next time you defrost, the ice will loosen quickly and drop off in sheets.

Wash inside and out with a mixture of 3 tablespoons of baking soda in a quart of warm water.

Sinks: For a sparkling white sink, place paper towels across the bottom of your sink and saturate with household bleach. Let set for 1/2 hour or so.

Rub stainless steel sinks with lighter fluid if rust marks appear. After the rust disappears wipe with your regular kitchen cleanser.

Use a cloth dampened with rubbing alcohol to remove water spots from stainless steel.

Spots on stainless steel can also be removed with white vinegar.

Club soda will shine up stainless steel sinks in a jiffy.

Teakettle: To remove lime deposits, fill with equal parts of vinegar and water. Bring to a boil and allow to stand overnight.

To unplug sink: Pour in one cup or more of white vinegar and a cup of baking soda, then add hot water out of the tap at full force. When bubbling stops, drain should be clear. Need no plumber.

Fingerprints off the kitchen door and walls: Take away fingerprints. Spot removal: Two parts water and one part rubbing alcohol are the basic ingredients in any commercial spot remover.

Dish Drainer: Remove hard water stains from your dish drainer by tilting the low end of the board slightly and pouring one cup of white vinegar over the board. Let it set overnight and rub off with a sponge in the morning.

Garbage disposal: Grind a half lemon or orange rind in the disposal to remove any unpleasant odor.

Clogged drains: When a drain is clogged with grease, pour a cup of salt and a cup of baking soda into the drain followed by a kettle of boiling water. The grease will usually dissolve immediately and open the drain.

Keeping Furniture Clean

To remove polish build-up: Mix 1/2 cup vinegar and 1/2 cup water. Rub with a soft cloth that has been moistened with solution, but wrung out. Dry immediately with another soft cloth.

Polishing carved furniture: Dip an old soft toothbrush into furniture polish and brush lightly.

Cigarette burns: For small minor burns, try rubbing mayonnaise into the burn. Let set for a while before wiping off with a soft cloth.

Burns can be repaired with a wax stick (available in all colors at paint and hardware stores). Gently scrape away the charred finish. Heat a knife blade and melt the shellac stick against the heated blade. Smooth over damaged area with your finger. But always consider the value of the furniture. It might be better to have a professional make the repair.

Or, make a paste of rottenstone (available at hardware stores) and salad oil. Rub into the burned spot only, following the grain of wood. Wipe clean with a cloth that has been dampened in oil. Wipe dry and apply your favorite furniture polish.

Removing paper that is stuck to a wood surface: Do not scrape with a knife. Pour any salad oil, a few drops at a time, on the paper. Let set for a while and rub with a soft cloth. Repeat the procedure until the paper is completely gone.

Old decals can be removed easily by painting them with several coats of white vinegar. Give the vinegar time to soak in, then gently scrape off.

Scratches: Make sure you always rub with the grain of the wood when repairing a scratch.

Walnut: Remove the meat from a fresh, unsalted walnut or pecan nut. Break it in half and rub the scratch with the broken side of the nut.

Mahogany: You can either rub the scratch with a dark brown crayon or buff with brown paste wax.

Red Mahogany: Apply ordinary iodine with a number 0 artist's brush.

Maple: Combine equal amounts of iodine and denatured alcohol. Apply with a Q-tip, then dry, wax and buff.

Ebony: Use black shoe polish, black eyebrow pencil or black crayon.

Teakwood: Rub very gently with 0000 steel wool. Rub in equal amounts of linseed oil and turpentine.

Light-finished furniture: Scratches can be hidden by using tan shoe polish. However, only on shiny finishes.

For all minor scratches: Cover each scratch with a generous amount of white petroleum jelly. Allow it to remain on for 24 hours. Rub into wood. Remove excess and polish as usual.

For larger scratches: Fill by rubbing with a wax stick (available in all colors at your hardware or paint store) or a crayon that matches the finish of the wood.

Three solutions to remove white water rings and spots: Dampen a soft cloth with water and put a dab of toothpaste on it. For stubborn stains, add baking soda to the toothpaste.

Make a paste of butter or mayonnaise and cigarette ashes. Apply to spot and buff away.

Apply a paste of salad oil and salt. Let stand briefly. Wipe and polish.

Marble table-top stains: Sprinkle salt on a fresh-cut lemon. Rub very lightly over stain. Do not rub hard or you will ruin the polished surface. Wash off with soap and water.

Scour with a water and baking soda paste. Let stand for a few minutes before rinsing with warm water.

Removing candle wax from wooden finishes: Soften the wax with a hair dryer. Remove wax with paper toweling and wash down with a solution of vinegar and water.

Plastic table tops: You will find that a coat of Turtle Wax is a quick pick-up for dulled plastic table tops and counters.
Or, rub in toothpaste and buff.

Glass table tops: Rub in a little lemon juice. Dry with paper towels and shine with newspaper for a sparkling table.
Toothpaste will remove small scratches from glass.

Chrome cleaning: For sparkling clean chrome without streaks, use a cloth dampened in ammonia.

Removing glue: Cement glue can be removed by rubbing with cold cream, peanut butter or salad oil.

Wicker: Wicker needs moisture, so use a humidifier in the winter.
To prevent drying out, apply lemon oil occasionally.
Never let wicker freeze. This will cause cracking and splitting.
Wash with a solution of warm salt water to keep from turning yellow.

Metal furniture: To remove rust, a good scrubbing with turpentine should accomplish this job.

Vinyl upholstery: Never oil vinyl as this will make it hard. It is almost impossible to soften again. For proper cleaning, sprinkle baking soda or vinegar on a rough, damp cloth, then wash with a mild dishwashing soap.

Soiled upholstery: Rub soiled cotton upholstery fabric with an artgum eraser or squares (purchased at stationery store).

Leather upholstery: Prevent leather from cracking by polishing regularly with a cream made of 1 part vinegar and 2 parts linseed oil. Clean with a damp cloth and saddle soap.

Grease stains: Absorb grease on furniture by pouring salt on the spill immediately.

Three solutions to remove white water rings and spots: Dampen a soft cloth with water and put a dab of toothpaste on it. For stubborn stains, add baking soda to the toothpaste.
Make a paste of butter or mayonnaise and cigarette ashes. Apply to spot and buff away.
Apply a paste of salad oil and salt. Let stand briefly. Wipe and polish.

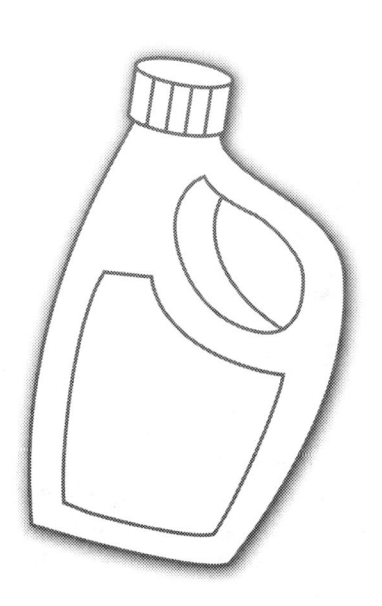

Laundry Care

Spot removal: Two parts water and one part rubbing alcohol are the basic ingredients in any commercial spot remover.

Clean machine: Fill your washer with warm water and add a gallon of distilled vinegar. Run the machine through the entire cycle to unclog and clean soap scum from hoses.

Too sudsy: When your washer overflows with too many suds, sprinkle salt in the water - the suds will disappear.

Hand-washed sweaters: Add a capful of hair cream rinse to the final rinse water when washing sweaters.

Whiter fabric: Linen or cotton can be whitened by boiling in a mixture or 1 part cream of tartar and 3 parts water.

Whitest socks: Boil socks in water to which a lemon slice has been added.

Freshen feather pillows: Put feather pillows in the dryer and tumble, then air outside.

Lintless corduroy: While corduroy is still damp, brush with clothes brush to remove all lint.

Ironing tip: When pressing pants, iron the top part on the wrong side. Iron the legs on the right side. This gives the pockets and waistband a smooth look.

Creaseless garments: Take an empty cardboard paper towel roll and cut through it lengthwise. Slip it over a wire hanger to prevent a crease from forming in the garment to be hung on the hanger.

Remove creases from hems: Sponge material with a white vinegar solution and press flat to remove creases in hems.

Bedroom ironing: A good place to iron is in the bedroom. Closets are nearby to hang clothes up immediately, and the bed makes a good surface on which to fold clothes and separate items into piles.

Ironing board cover: When washing your ironing board cover, attach it to the board while it is still damp. When it dries, the surface will be completely smooth.

Starch your ironing board cover. This helps the cover stay clean longer.

Lint remover: Add a yard of nylon netting to your dryer with the wet clothes - it will catch most of the lint.

Washer advice: Button all buttons on clothing and turn inside out before putting into the washer. Fewer buttons will fall off and garments will fade less if turned inside out.

Soiled collars: Use a small paintbrush and brush hair shampoo into soiled shirt collars before laundering. Shampoo is made to dissolve body oils.

Faster ironing: Place a strip of heavy-duty aluminum foil over the entire length of the ironing board and cover with pad. As you iron, heat will reflect through the underside of the garment.

Ironing embroidery: Lay the embroidery piece upside-down on a Turkish towel before ironing. All the little spaces between the embroidery will be smooth when you are finished.

Removing Stains from Washables

Alcoholic beverages: Pre-soak or sponge fresh stains immediately with cold water, then with cold water and glycerin. Rinse with vinegar for a few seconds if stain remains. These stains may turn brown with age. If wine stain remains, rub with concentrated detergent; wait 15 minutes; rinse. Repeat if necessary. Wash with detergent in hottest water safe for fabric.

Baby Food: Use liquid laundry detergent and brush into stain with an old toothbrush then wash.

Blood: Pre-soak in cold or warm water at least 30 minutes. If stain remains, soak in lukewarm ammonia water (3 tablespoons per gallon water). Rinse. If stain remains, work in detergent, and wash, using bleach safe for fabric.

Candle wax: Use a dull knife to scrape off as much as possible. Place fabric between 2 blotters or facial tissues and press with warm iron. Remove color stain with non-flammable dry cleaning solvent. Wash with detergent in the hottest water safe for fabric.

Chewing gum: Rub area with ice, then scrape off with a dull blade. Sponge with dry cleaning solvent; allow to air dry. Wash in detergent and hottest water safe for fabric.

Cosmetics: Loosen stain with a non-flammable dry cleaning solvent. Rub detergent in until stain outline is gone. Wash in hottest water and detergent safe for fabric.

Deodorants: Sponge area with white vinegar. If stain remains, soak with denatured alcohol. Wash with detergent in hottest water safe for fabric.

Dye: If dye transfers from a non-colorfast item during washing, immediately bleach discolored items. Repeat as necessary BEFORE drying. On whites use color remover. CAUTION: Do not use color remover in washer, or around washer and dryer as it may damage the finish.

Fruit and fruit juices: Sponge with cold water. Pre-soak in cold or warm water for at least 30 minutes. Wash with detergent and bleach safe for fabric.

Grass: Pre-soak in cold water for at least 30 minutes. Rinse. Pre-treat with detergent, hot water, and bleach safe for fabric. On acetate and colored fabrics, use 1 part of alcohol to 2 parts water.

Grease, oil, tar or butter: Method 1: Use powder or chalk absorbents to remove as much grease as possible. Pre-treat with detergent or non-flammable dry cleaning solvent, or liquid shampoo. Wash in hottest water safe for fabric, using plenty of detergent.
Method 2: Rub spot with lard and sponge with a non-flammable dry cleaning solvent. Wash in hottest water and detergent safe for fabric.

Perspiration: Sponge fresh stain with ammonia; old stain with vinegar. Pre-soak in cold or warm water. Rinse. Wash in hottest water safe for fabric. If fabric is yellowed, use bleach. If stain still remains, dampen and sprinkle with meat tenderizer, or pepsin. Let stand 1 hour. Brush off and wash. For persistent odor, sponge with colorless mouthwash.

Ketchup or Mustard: Scrape excess. Use commercial spot remover. Rinse; launder.

Mud: Let stain dry. Brush off; launder. Tough stain: Soak in cool water for 30 minutes; work liquid laundry detergent into stain; rinse.

Milk, cream, ice cream: Pre-soak in cold or warm water for 30 minutes. Wash. Sponge any grease spots with non-flammable dry cleaning solvent. Wash again.

Household Hints - 7

Removing Stains from Carpets & Floors

Candle drippings: For spilled wax on carpet, use a brown paper bag as a blotter and run a hot iron over it, which will absorb the wax.

Dog stains: Blot up excess moisture with paper towel. Pour club soda on the spot and continue blotting. Lay a towel over the spot and set a heavy object on top in order to absorb all the moisture.

Rug care: When washing and drying foam-backed throw rugs, never wash in hot water, and use the "air only" dryer setting to dry. Heat will ruin foam.

Cleaning rugs: If the rug is only slightly dirty, you can clean it with cornmeal. Use a stiff brush to work the cornmeal into the pile of the rug. Take it all out with the vacuum.

Spills on the rug: When spills happen, go to the bathroom and grab a can of shaving cream. Squirt it on the spot then rinse off with water.

Ballpoint ink marks: Saturate the spots with hairspray. Allow to dry. Brush lightly with a solution of water and vinegar.

Glue: Glue can be loosened by saturating the spot with a cloth soaked in vinegar.

Repairing braided rugs: Braided rugs often rip apart. Instead of sewing them, use clear fabric glue to repair. It's that fast and easy.

Repairing a burn: Remove some fuzz from the carpet, either by shaving or pulling out with a tweezer. Roll into the shape of the burn. Apply a good cement glue to the backing of the rug and press the fuzz down into the burned spot. Cover with a piece of cleansing tissue and place a heavy book on top. This will cause the glue to dry very slowly and will get the best results.

Spot remover for outdoor carpeting: Spray spots liberally with a pre-wash commercial spray. Let it set several minutes, then hose down and watch the spots disappear.

Blood on the rug: When you get blood on your rug, rub off as much as you can at first, then take a cloth soaked in cold water and wet the spot, wiping it up as you go. If a little bit remains, pour some ammonia onto the cool, wet cloth and lightly wipe that over the spot, too. Rinse it right away with cold water.

Crayon Marks: Use silver polish to remove from vinyl tile or linoleum.

Spilled nail polish: Allow to almost dry, then peel off of waxed floors or tile.

Tar spots: Use paste wax to remove tar from floors. Works on shoes, too.

Dusting floors: Stretch a nylon stocking over the dust mop. After using, discard the stocking and you will have a clean mop.

Varnished floors: Use cold tea to clean woodwork and varnished floors.

Spilled grease: Rub floor with ice cubes to solidify grease. Scrape up excess and wash with soapy water.

Quick shine: Put a piece of waxed paper under your dust mop. Dirt will stick to the mop and the wax will shine your floors.

Unmarred floors: Put thick old socks over the legs of heavy furniture when moving across floors.

Wood floor care: Never use water or water-based cleaners on wood floors. Over a period of time, warping and swelling will develop.

Heel marks: Just take a pencil eraser and wipe them off.

Floor polisher: When cleaning the felt pads of your floor polisher, place the pads between layers of newspaper and press with an iron to absorb built-up wax.

Garage floors: In an area where a large amount of oil has spilled, lay several thicknesses of newspaper. Saturate the paper with water; press flat against the floor. When dry, remove the newspaper and the spots will have disappeared.

Basement floors: Sprinkle sand on oily spots, let it absorb the oil, and sweep up.

Basic Fabric Care

Keep your clothing and fabrics looking and feeling great by following a few basic washing, drying and ironing rules. Be sure to follow any specific instructions on the care label of clothing pieces. Take tailored clothes and special items to a dry cleaner.

Fabric	Washing	Drying & Ironing
Acetates	Machine or hand wash at a low temperature. Do not wring or fast spin in machine.	Line dry naturally and iron while damp. Use a pressing cloth to protect fabric.
Acrylic	Usually machine washable - check label. Wash at low temperature.	Dry flat, line dry or use a sweater rack. Do not tumble dry.
Brocade	Hand wash at cool temperature or dry clean. Do not wring.	Do not tumble dry. Allow acetate items to dry naturally and iron while still damp.
Cashmere	Hand wash in cool water in well-dissolved soap. Rinse well. Do not wring.	Pull into shape after washing and remove excess water. Dry flat or line dry.
Corduroy	Always wash inside out. Hand or machine wash -check label.	Iron on the wrong side over a towel.
Cotton	Machine wash at high temperature, separating whites from colors.	Dry and gently pull into shape. Iron inside out while damp with a cool iron.
Denim	Wash separately until there is no color run. Wash items inside out.	Iron inside out while evenly damp. Smooth fabric with a soft cloth.
Leather & Suede	Protect items with leather spray after hand washing.	Tumble or line dry. Iron before items are completely dry.
Linen	Machine wash according to label.	Tumble or line dry. Iron while very damp with a hot iron.
Silk	Hand wash in warm water. Some items may be machine washed on delicate cycle.	Rub suede onto another piece of suede or use a suede brush.
Wool	Hand wash unless machine is acceptable - check label.	Iron while damp. Starch to prevent creases.

Food Safety

Keep your family and yourself healthy by ensuring the foods you consume have been purchased, stored and prepared safely. A general understanding of how germs and bacteria grow will help protect you and your family from the risk of food poisoning.

When shopping:
- Carefully check over fresh fruits and vegetables for bruising, rotting or discoloration.
- Try to keep chilled and frozen foods as cold as possible between buying these items and storage at home. Once home, transfer these foods to the refrigerator or freezer immediately.
- Read all package labels carefully, noting the expiration date and any ingredients that may affect a family member by causing an allergic reaction.

When storing:
- Make sure your refrigerator is running correctly and kept cold enough, as harmful bacteria will flourish in warmer temperatures. Keep the coldest part of the refrigerator around 0 to 5°C/32 to 41°F.
- Store the most perishable foods in the coldest part of the refrigerator.
- Place foods that should be kept cooler, such as milk, fruit juices, cheeses, butter and eggs, in the refrigerator's special compartments.
- Wrap and cover all raw and uncooked foods to prevent them from touching other foods.
- Discard foods that have been kept longer than the "use by" or "best before" date.

When preparing:
- Keep your hands and all equipment extremely clean.
- Never use a knife that has been used to cut raw meat or fish for anything else before washing it thoroughly.
- Use separate cutting boards for raw foods, vegetables and cooked meats.
- Carefully wash and disinfect cutting boards, counter surfaces and kitchen towels after all uses.
- High temperatures will kill most bacteria. Be sure to cook foods throughout, especially raw meats and fish. A good rule of thumb is to cook meats so the center reaches 70°C/158°F for at least 2 minutes.
- Cooking raw eggs will destroy bacteria. Avoid recipes calling for uncooked eggs.
- It is best to thaw frozen foods in the refrigerator or microwave. If frozen meats or fish are not completely thawed, the center may not cook properly.
- Never reheat food or meals more than once.

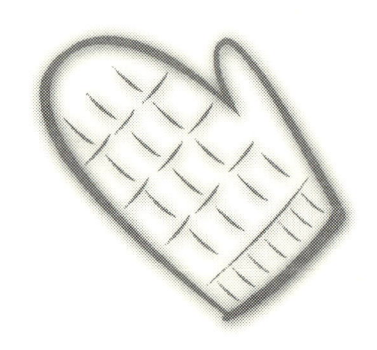

Kitchen Safety

Kitchen Fires:
Always keep a domestic fire extinguisher in the kitchen. However, be careful not to position the extinguisher above the stove, as a stovetop or oven fire would make the extinguisher inaccessible. Be sure to train your entire family on how to use the fire extinguisher. A compact fire blanket kept close will help suffocate flames from deep-fat fryers, which are a major cause of household fires. NEVER throw water on grease fires!

Hygiene:
Always wash hands in warm soapy water before touching food, after touching raw foods and before touching ready-to-eat foods. If cuts or scrapes occur while cooking food, be sure to wash and cover the area immediately. Wipe hands on a separate kitchen towel, reserving the dish towel for dishes only. Bleach, disinfect or replace kitchen towels, cloths and sponges often, especially after working with raw foods. Return perishable foods, such as butter or milk, to the refrigerator as soon as possible after use.

Child Safety:
Use cupboard lock handles so children and infants cannot get into harmful kitchen chemicals or other products. Buy detergents and cleaning chemicals that have child-proof lids or store these products in high cupboards or on high shelves that are out of reach. Never leave knives or scissors on the counter. Try to keep them out of the way by placing them in a lockable drawer, on a magnetic rack or in a wooden knife block.

Hot Pans:
On the stovetop, make sure pan handles are pointing inwards so they won't be knocked off or catch on loose clothing. When using a frying pan, place a splatter guard over the pan so you or others will not be splattered by hot oil or grease.

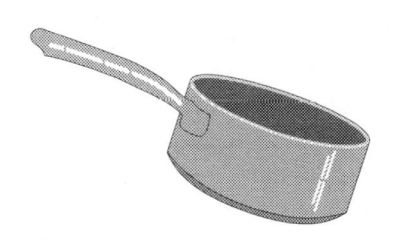

Perfect Party Checklist

✔ Create the party guest list.

✔ If applicable, pick a party theme. Party themes can be helpful during the planning process, as they give the party a defined purpose and focus.

✔ As party ideas come to you, jot them down. Don't rely on your memory for thoughts and inspiration.

✔ Create/buy invitations and send. If you have a theme, use the invitations to incorporate the theme and as a way to get party guests excited for the event!

✔ Gather materials needed for serving food, party games, decorations, music and/or party favors.

✔ Create the party menu, including snacks, main meal, beverages and/or dessert.

✔ Buy all necessary food and ingredients. If possible, prepare as much food the day before or morning of the party. If necessary, chill the beverages.

✔ Set the mood with decorations, lighting and music.

✔ Don't forget to wear something that is comfortable but, as the party host, makes you feel special!

✔ Set out party snacks, beverages, decorations and favors.

✔ Relax and welcome your guests!

Menu Planning

When selecting recipes for a party:
- Plan the main course first, unless a meal will not be served. After choosing the main course, pick appetizers, sides and desserts to complement it.
- Keep the courses simple and try to choose items that can be either entirely or partly prepared ahead of time.
- Try to create a balance of color, texture and flavor throughout the courses. Avoid choosing recipes that are too similar, for example, all egg- or cheese-based.
- Balance a rich or spicy dish with a plain, light and/or refreshing appetizer or dessert.
- Be aware of any special dietary or allergic requirements your guests may have.
- Unless you have extra help, try to limit the amount of courses to three.

Estimating Quantities

Food	10 Portions	20 Portions	40 Portions
Soup	1/2 gallon	1 gallon	2 gallons
Cold, sliced meats	2 lbs.	3 lbs. 14 oz.	7 lbs. 11 oz.
Boneless meat for casseroles	2 lbs. 3 oz.	5 lbs.	10 lbs.
Roast meat on the bone	3 lbs. 14 oz.	6 lbs. 10 oz.	14 lbs. 5 oz.
Cheese	12 oz.	2 lbs.	2 lbs. 12 oz.
Crackers for cheese	1 lb. 1 oz.	1 lb. 10 oz.	2 lbs. 3 oz.
Filleted fish	2 lbs. 12 oz.	5 lbs.	10 lbs.
Whole chicken or turkey	7 lbs. 11 oz.	15 lbs. 7 oz.	2 x 7 lbs. 11 oz.
Rice or pasta (uncooked weight)	1 lb. 1 oz.	1 lb. 9 oz.	2 lbs. 12 oz.
Fresh fruits or fruit salad	3 lbs. 5 oz.	6 lbs. 1 oz.	12 lbs. 2 oz.
Ice cream	1/2 gallon	3/4 gallon	1 1/4 gallons

Table Settings

For a Full-Course Meal

- Large goblet for red wine
- Dessert spoon laid above dessert fork
- Water glass
- Small wine glass for white wine
- Plate set for first course
- Butter knife
- Napkin placed on side plate
- Forks to left of plate in order of use from left
- Knives and spoon to right of plate, knife blades toward plate

For a Casual Meal

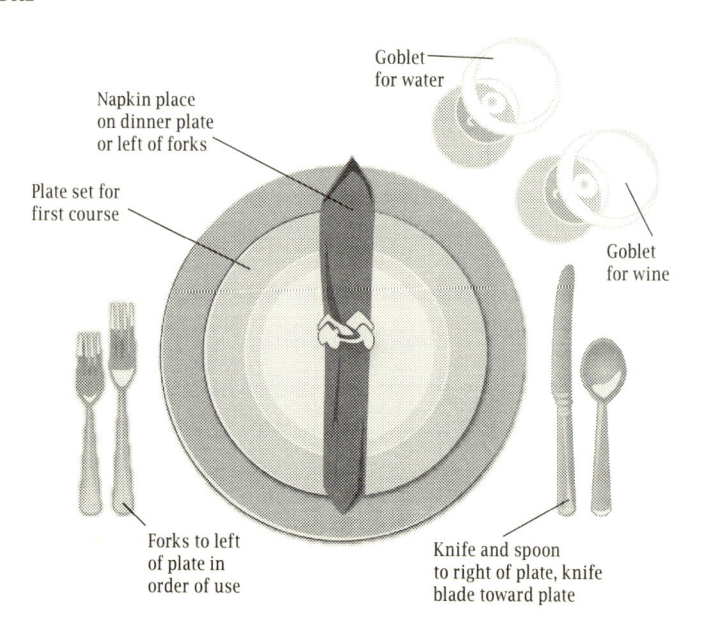

- Goblet for water
- Napkin place on dinner plate or left of forks
- Plate set for first course
- Goblet for wine
- Forks to left of plate in order of use
- Knife and spoon to right of plate, knife blade toward plate

14 - Household Hints

Buffet Arrangement

Arranging the Buffet Table:
- Decide which direction guests will walk around the table.
- Start with empty plates, then side dishes, followed by the main dish and finally the vegetables and salads. Place serving utensils beside each dish.
- Set breads, relishes, cutlery and napkins at the end of the table. If there is room, set decorations in the center of the table.
- Leave room behind the buffet table so you have easy access for replacing dishes.
- Leave spaces between dishes on the buffet table so guests can set down glasses or plates when serving themselves.
- To keep cold side dishes or salads chilled, set the serving bowl or dish inside a separate dish that is full of ice.
- Place drinks, glasses, cups and ice on a separate table to avoid congestion in one area.

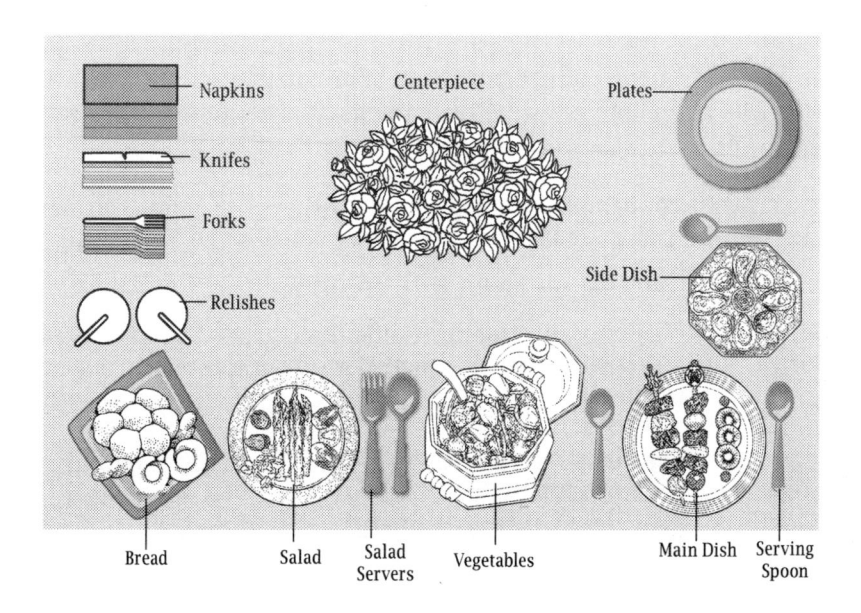

Staying Organized

Use the following tips to keep your home organized:

- Use drawer dividers to give smaller items a well-defined spot. Within the drawers, store very small items in jewelry boxes, ice cube trays, desk trays, etc.

- Label storage containers or boxes with pictures or words so everyone will know the contents within. Color-coding works well, too. Color-code items for certain areas. For example, yellow-tagged items go in the upstairs bathroom. Or, use a separate color for each family member. For instance, Donna's color is red and Kathi's color is blue.

- Store items close to where they are used. For example, store jumper cables in the car trunk, pens and paper close to the phone and fast-food coupons in the car.

- Keep separate folders holding data for the home, for each car, for pets and for tax and insurance documents.

- Use a file folder to hold receipts for valuable items. File any guarantees or warranties together with the appropriate receipt.

- Print hard copies of important documents on your computer and file the documents in a safe place. This will allow you to retrieve the documents in case the computer breaks down or is stolen.

- If you keep magazines or pamphlets that do not show their title or issue on the spine, group the items by title and sort in a magazine file. Place a label on the file showing the contents within.

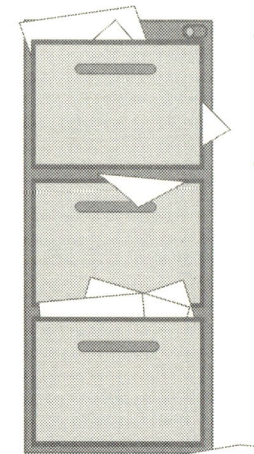

- Combine all cleaning fluids, detergents and rags needed to clean a particular area or room. Place them together in a sturdy container or bucket.

- Use lists to remember items needed, important errands or appointments. If possible, carry the list with you and check the items off as they are gathered or completed.

How to Order

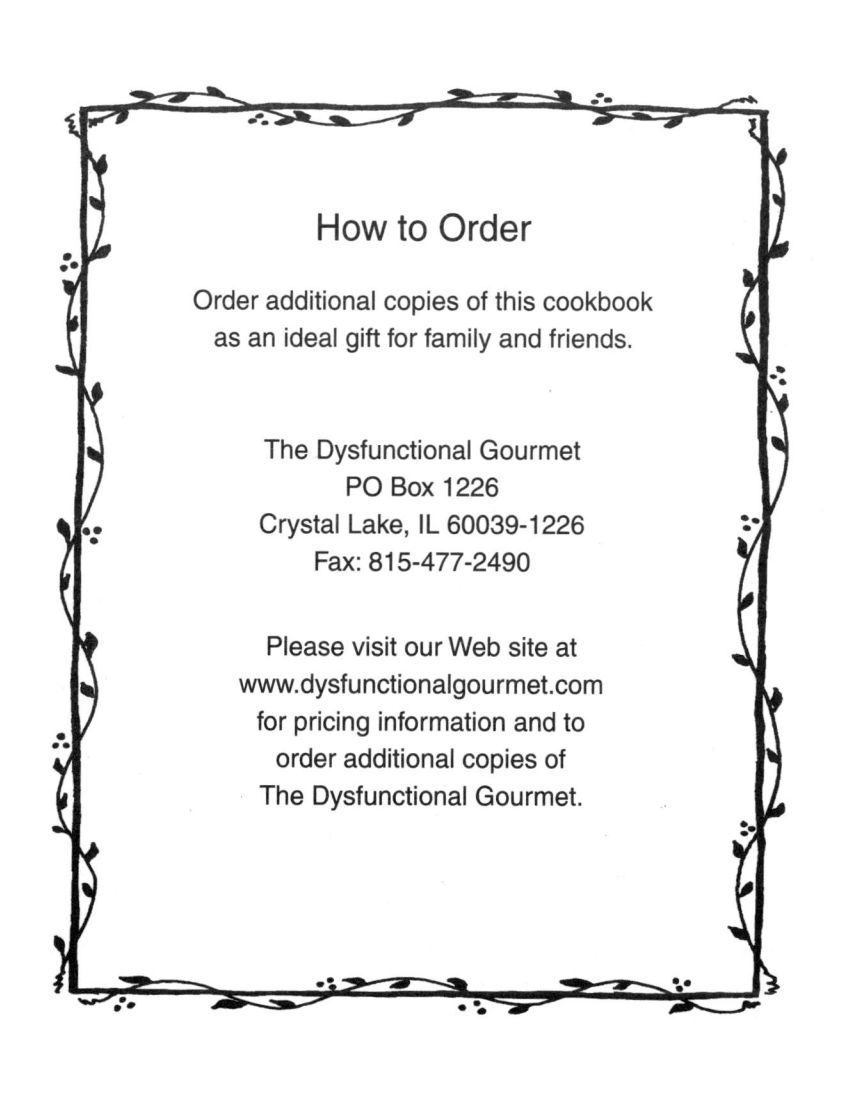

Order additional copies of this cookbook as an ideal gift for family and friends.

The Dysfunctional Gourmet
PO Box 1226
Crystal Lake, IL 60039-1226
Fax: 815-477-2490

Please visit our Web site at
www.dysfunctionalgourmet.com
for pricing information and to
order additional copies of
The Dysfunctional Gourmet.